WHAT'S YOUR WORD?

Choosing Your Path One Word at a Time

By Kevin White

International *Bestselling Author*

WHAT'S YOUR WORD?

Choosing Your Path One Word at a Time

KEVIN WHITE

What's Your Word?

Choosing Your Path One Word at a Time

2022© by Kevin White

All rights reserved. Published 2022.

BIBLE SCRIPTURES

Printed in the United States of America

Spirit Media

www.spiritmedia.us

Spirit Media and our logos are trademarks of Spirit Media

1249 Kildaire Farm Rd STE 112

Cary, NC 27511

1 (888) 800-3744

Religion & Spirituality | Christian Books & Bibles | Spiritual Growth

Paperback ISBN: 978-1-958304-12-9

Hardback ISBN: 978-1-958304-13-6

Audiobook ISBN: 978-1-958304-14-3

eBook ISBN: 978-1-958304-06-8

Library of Congress Control Number: 2022917722

SPIRIT MEDIA

Register This New Book

Benefits of Registering*

- FREE **replacements** of lost or damaged books
- FREE **audiobook**—Get to the Point by Kevin White
- FREE information about new titles and other **freebies**

www.spiritmedia.us/register

*See our website for requirements and limitations

TABLE OF CONTENTS

INTRODUCTION

I had no idea about the power of taking action on one single word.

ONE SINGLE WORD

My first trip to India in 1998 was a life changing experience for me. I'd been in full-time Christian ministry as a pastor for ten years. As an entrepreneur and church planter, I knew all the church growth strategies.

I would read Psalm 127:1 (NLT), "Unless the Lord builds a house, the work of the builders is wasted." I'd then go to leadership conferences and be told, "If it is to be, it's up to me." My forty-hour work week became sixty, eighty, even ninety hours a week. The expectation I put on myself to do great things for God nearly killed me.

In India, I saw churches in thatch roof huts without bulletins, budgets, or Bibles. They didn't have all the church growth resources we have in the USA. All they had was a passionate pursuit for the presence of God. There was an undeniable sense of God's presence in their midst.

Every believer shared stories of how God had miraculously healed someone, provided, or revealed himself. They literally had nothing of material possession compared to Christians in the USA, yet they exhibited pure joy and genuine gratitude to the Lord.

I was so convicted. I knew I wanted what they had. I had pursued so many good things for God in my life and ministry. I pursued impact, influence, and fruit for God. In fact, I had become such a workaholic for God it nearly killed me and my family. In India it hit me. I'd been pursuing everything except the presence of God.

On the plane ride back I committed to passionately pursue the presence of God every day for the rest of my life. That is when everything began to change. It took years to understand the significance of that decision. I look back on that plane ride and know God focused my attention on one single word...

PRESENCE

Obviously, God's PRESENCE.

Just like that, He completely rewrote my job description to a single word: PRESENCE. I had a degree in theology. My whole life revolved around Christian ministry. Just like that God rewrote my complete philosophy of ministry to be one single word: PRESENCE.

Obviously, other words like "passionately" and "pursue" were significant too, but neither made any difference without the word "PRESENCE."

As I wrote about in my book, *Get to the Point: Every Guidance and Provision You Will Ever Need Can Be Found Today in God's Presence,* God gave me the one single word that day: PRESENCE, which changed the trajectory of my life even more than being saved.

COURAGE

At the end of 2019, God gave me the word COURAGE as a prayer and focus word for my life for 2020. As you can imagine, Covid-19 caused me to appreciate God's word of COURAGE all throughout 2020. Actually, I had no idea how much COURAGE it was going to take to write my first book until I started writing it in January of 2020. The word COURAGE and actual courage have become incredible gifts from God. COURAGE is now a spiritual marker in my life. I wrote about COURAGE in my first book, *Audacious Generosity*. It all started with one single word.

CATCH

In 2021, God gave me a word, CATCH, from Luke 5 as a prayer word or focus word for my life. It brought an expectation of miracles as in miraculous CATCH. In February, I was focused on marketing my new book and God asked me, "What if I want you to write your second book now?" I had thought maybe in three years. I surrendered the marketing of *Audacious Generosity* to God and began writing book #2.

A few months later I was writing book #2 and sharing about the word PRESENCE, and it was as if God took me aside and, in an instant, showed me book #3—this book: *What's Your Word?* Actually, I saw multiple books. That's CATCH.

When I went to publish book #2, *Get To The Point*, God guided me to start a new publishing company: Spirit Media, which I launched in

November 2021. My aim was to create a new company that will reinvent Christian publishing. I could fill up a book with the guidance God has given me for Spirit Media. That's CATCH!

For the past twelve years I've served as the founder/executive director of Global Hope India. There are over 1 billion people in India who have never held a Bible. We believe everyone should have access to know about Jesus. We empower pastors in India with short-term missions and needed resources from the USA.

I've been to India over fifty times, taking 1,000 people on short-term mission trips. That is a result of passionately pursuing God's PRESENCE.

When the Covid-19 pandemic happened, we couldn't travel to India anymore. That's when God gave me the word: COURAGE. Instead of traveling I wrote. For over twenty years God had shown me the power of audacious generosity to open doors for the gospel. In fact, God's strategy has always been audacious generosity (John 3:16).

After ten years of traveling to India four out of twelve months a year, God gave me the word CATCH.

Right after New Year's 2022, God prompted me to calculate all the donations to Global Hope India from people who were not regular donors prior to having been given complimentary copies of my books. It totaled $150,000 of which $112,000 was from first-time donors who had not previously given to Global Hope India. That's CATCH!

God has given unexpected properties, businesses, relationships, and breakthroughs. I could go on and on about all the manifestations of the word CATCH in my life, our family, and Global Hope India.

FILL

As soon as I asked God for a word for 2022, he immediately brought the word FILL into my spirit. Specifically, the promise that he will FILL. It is a continuation of the word CATCH. It bears a very specific expectation that God will FILL. It's a promise for my life, our family, Global Hope India, Spirit Media, and beyond.

When we upgraded to larger refrigerators in two of our properties, God said, FILL. When our son and his wife closed on a second home, God said, FILL. When Pastor Resources featured me in a video to over 100,000 pastors, God said, FILL. I could give specific examples about my books, Spirit Media, Global Hope India, and even our partners in India.

What's Your Word? will help you unleash the power of God in your life as you activate one single word at a time.

PAINT BY NUMBERS

When I was growing up, I loved doing paint by number kits. Each kit would come with a tray of about ten different colors of paint. Each color was a number, one through ten. The kit also contained a paint brush and a canvas board with a sketch on it that was divided into various sections. Each section had a number.

The instructions were simple. Paint all sections marked #1 with the paint labeled #1, then proceed doing the same with colors two through ten.

When you finish painting all the #1 sections with #1 paint, the canvas doesn't look too good. Each color added completes the canvas a little more. When all ten colors are added then the beautiful art piece is revealed.

So it is with *What's Your Word?*

Each chapter focuses on one significant word. Each word builds upon the previous word. By the end of the book, we will have a beautiful piece of art.

By the end of each chapter, you'll appreciate and value the word for that chapter. When you finish reading the book, you'll understand the significance of asking the question, "What's your word?" You'll be comfortable asking God for His word for your life. You'll know your word and how to help others know their word.

Each chapter reveals many great words.

The English Bible contains approximately 785,000 words. Every word from God is precious and needs to be cherished. The challenge is savoring God's word, one word at a time. Unfortunately, I know from personal experience that it is possible to rush through God's word and miss the importance of single words. *What's Your Word?* will help you notice, appreciate, and activate single words. If you're already doing that it will affirm you and stretch you with new and exciting words.

LEARNING TO ENJOY EVERY BITE

I grew up poor. As a result I learned to eat fast. With a family of six and not a lot of food sometimes I learned that the faster I ate the more I got. This became a really bad habit for me. It has taken a lot of time and discipline for me to learn to enjoy individual bites. I had to work hard to savor one bite at a time.

Through the years I've learned to take smaller bites, put my fork down, and chew slower. As I've done that, individual bites have made tastes come alive. God's word says, "Taste and see that the Lord is good." (Psalm 34:8 NTL). Let's allow God to teach us to taste. If we aren't careful, it is possible to swallow and digest without ever tasting. God is so awesome. He is so creative. He loves us so much. He wants us to taste. He is worthy of us tasting.

Tasting involves identifying specific ingredients. Perhaps you love the taste of chocolate, coffee, fruits, vanilla, and more!

In the same way, tasting God's word involves identifying specific words God wants to speak over you. Words He wants you to hear, take seriously, and obey. Words from which He wants you to reap the benefits. Words He wants to use to bless your socks off.

As you'll see, God created individual words with momentum, and as we engage these words and their momentum, God fulfills His word in our lives.

God doesn't only ask us to obey Him. He asks us to imitate Him. As we allow His Holy Spirit to live in and through us, we become a reflection of God. In *What's Your Word?* you'll see how you can literally choose your path with a single word.

As King of Kings and Lord of Lords, God is The Master Communicator. He offers the ultimate "Master Class." He always starts with why. He has masterfully created and chosen each word He uses. He created you, loves you, and has prepared a very specific word for your life.

As you will see, God offers you the choice of words. Some words lead to disaster. Other words lead to prosperity. You choose your path. God is able to prosper you and everyone else with one single word. God is All powerful and He created words with power. Since Genesis 1, God has been accomplishing everything He speaks. God says it and it's done—one word at a time.

In fact, I'm going to show you how to choose God's path of prosperity for your life. You'll be able to use this in your life, family, business, church, and nonprofit.

In ten chapters I show you ten very powerful words:

1. ONE
2. DISASTER

3. PROSPERITY

4. COLLISION

5. VISION

6. VALUE

7. WHY

8. NOISE

9. EVERYONE

10. WORD

When you begin to speak, use, and harness these words, you will witness firsthand the miraculous power of God in your life. This is only the beginning. This will train you in the power of a single word. Once you've finished the book you'll have all you need to identify and harness other words for God's glory and mission.

Each one of us desperately needs to understand all we can about the words God has spoken over our lives, and how to activate them. Each word is a true gift from God that He wants you to receive and benefit from for His glory.

It all starts with appreciating the word ONE.

CHAPTER 1

Now listen! Today I am giving you a choice between life and death, between prosperity and disaster.

- Deuteronomy 30:15 (NLT)

You get ONE.

Only ONE.

When I was in third grade, Mrs. Hawkins gave everyone a peppermint stick. When I received mine I asked for another ONE. She took back the one she gave me, broke it in half, and gave it back to me. She said, "Now you have two." I was disappointed because I knew I still had only ONE.

In Deuteronomy 30 God is offering His people and you ONE choice.

He says, you have to pick ONE:

1. Life

or

2. Death

That's it. You have two choices. You must pick only ONE.

You can't die and continue to live. You can't live and be dead at the same time. You're either dead or alive. You're either going to continue to live or you're going to die.

You must pick ONE.

ONE word.

Throughout *What's Your Word?* I'm going to show you how God wants you to appreciate and focus on ONE individual word at a time. I'm going to be asking you what's your word? If you're already comfortable with this, then let this affirm you and let God reveal even more to you. If you're not comfortable with this, then join the club. I wasn't either. I used to know thousands of words while never appreciating the power of ONE word from God.

God could have said, "Let me give you a textbook on life and another ONE on death," but He didn't. He didn't give you a thick book to read, a paragraph or even a sentence. God gives you two words:

1. Life

or

2. Death

And says, "Pick ONE."

You can pick only ONE.

You must indicate your choice with ONE word:

1. Life

or

2. Death

What's Your Word?

You get ONE word. Remember, God isn't looking for a thick book back from you, a paragraph, or a sentence. He is waiting for you to choose ONE word. You get to respond with ONE word.

We don't get to say, "Well, God, it's complicated."
Or, "Well, God, it depends upon the day."
Or, "Can I wait until I'm 22 to decide?"
Or, "Let's talk this out for a while."

Nope.

God has given you a choice, asked you to pick ONE word, and you get to reply with only ONE word.

So, what's your Word?

This book is all about allowing God to boil down His guidance, call, purpose, and plan for your life to ONE single word at a time.

In 1998, my word from God became PRESENCE. After being a Christian over twenty years, I finally committed to passionately pursue the presence of God first and foremost for the rest of my life. My earlier book, *Get to the Point*, shares a small glimpse of what I've learned since then. I'm still learning.

Using thousands of words but never hearing God speak ONE specific word over your life is a tragedy.

SAVORING A SINGLE WORD

The King James Bible (KJV) has 783,137 words. The New International Bible (NIV) has 727,969 words. [1]

What's Your Word? is not about ignoring other words. It is about savoring a single word. There is a difference. Both are beneficial in every healthy relationship.

Good parenting involves moments when no other words matter except words like:

- No
- Stop
- Don't
- Come
- Stay

Good marriages involve moments when no other words matter except:

- Love
- Marry
- Baby
- Only
- Anniversary

Good employment involves critical words like:

- Hired
- Raise
- Congratulations
- Promotion
- Retirement

The examples are endless.

The same is true with God.

What's Your Word? is all about choosing your path ONE word at a time.

LIFE IS FOUNDATIONAL

Obviously the ONE word, life, is not God's only word. But it is a very foundational word. All other words don't matter once life ends. Just imagine talking to a deceased person you don't know. It doesn't matter how many words you use, they are no longer listening. You can speak thousands of words for ten hours straight. You'll still get no response. Life is foundational.

God's ONE word is "life." And it is a matter of life or death. It is so important that God has given us the answer key in Deuteronomy 30:19 (NLT):

> Today I have given you the choice between life and death,
> between blessings and curses. Now I call on heaven and earth
> to witness the choice you make. Oh, that you would choose life,
> so that you and your descendants might live!

Not only does God require us to pick only ONE:

1. Life

or

2. Death

He also pleads with us to choose life.

Think back to the sin of Adam and Eve in the Garden of Eden. The consequences of their rebellion can be summed up in ONE single word: choice.

Before, God's presence was automatic. After Adam and Eve rebelled against God, God's presence was a choice. As soon as we die, the choice is over. We either die in Christ or apart from Christ. Before we can choose God's presence, we must choose life. Then because we chose life, we can choose God's presence.

As we enter into a living and loving relationship with God through Jesus Christ, other critical words will come from God:

- Come
- Loved
- Mine
- Chosen
- Favored
- Blessed
- Go
- Serve
- Others

At the same time, you will want to respond to God with some invaluable words:

- Holy
- Lord
- Worship
- Love
- Surrender

- Give
- Praise
- Thanks

It all starts with ONE single word: life.

God gave you life and asks you to choose to live. You can reject this gift of life. You can choose death instead. That's your right.

But God is begging you to choose life. He has given you the choice and is looking for you to respond with only ONE word.

You get only ONE word.

LIFE IS A FIGHT

It is important for you to understand that you were born into a broken and sinful world with a propensity for death. While life is absolutely possible, you have to fight to stay alive. It doesn't take much to die. You can play on the road and easily die if you choose.

It's harder to live than to die.

Life isn't a joke. Life isn't a casual game we play. It takes effort to live. You have to maintain certain hygiene in order to stay healthy. You have to eat right, exercise, and avoid harmful chemicals in order to stay alive.

You'll need to drink lots of water and not antifreeze. You have to eat vegetables instead of rocks. You can't walk out into oncoming traffic or touch high voltage wires if you want to live.

Every year we hear about the same tragic automobile accident. You know the ONE. Where a car full of teenagers collides with a bridge, tree, or another car while traveling at excessive speed without wearing seat belts. Just like that, in the blink of an eye, young innocent lives are lost. Usually weeks before high school graduation. Grief counselors are brought into the school to help grieving classmates deal with the tragedy.

It doesn't take much to die. It takes more to stay alive. You have to choose to live.

Suicide is easy. Staying alive is hard. While we have to choose life, it does not have to be a battle.

If you struggle with contemplating suicide, please get help. In the US now you can even dial 988. Don't battle alone. There is hope. God wouldn't say, "now choose life" if it weren't possible.

The fact is there are evil forces of darkness fighting against you to live, but greater is Almighty God within you than he who is in the world. Those who Jesus sets free are truly free indeed (John 8:36). There is victory in Jesus.

LIFE IS WHAT YOU MAKE IT

Sadly, I've learned from mentoring many different people that some people don't want help. Oh, they whine alright. To them the battle is real. They can describe the struggle again and again and again. Unfortunately, they never do anything about it.

It's like a person with a broken arm who never goes to see a doctor. They never get the break reset. They don't get a cast. They don't allow the break to heal. They just go through life mourning their broken arm. Every day they see that their arm is broken. They are aware that they can't put much pressure on this arm. It hurts to lift their arm. They are unable to carry anything. So, instead of going and getting it fixed they just whine.

Now they get attention. People notice them. Everyone who sees their arm asks about it. The person gets to relive the accident that caused the break. They receive sympathy and pity. They also receive lots of advice about how to fix the arm, but they choose instead to live with it. Tomorrow will be the same as today. It's broken and nothing is going to fix it. Their life is just reduced to a life of pain and misery.

While this is a fictitious exaggeration, it is all too common. We all know people who don't want help. Perhaps you're ONE. I hope not. The truth is that life is what you and God make together!

While the reality of victimization is true, it's not forever. Every day unfortunate things happen where people are victimized. Bad things do happen to good people. Some extreme examples are terrorism, rape, murder, robbery, car jackings, and kidnappings. Assaults come in all shapes and sizes. I've had my share of verbal, physical, and mental assaults. It's a reality of life.

When I was growing up, my father lacked the skills to demonstrate his love. When he would get angry, he would yell, "Kevin, you'll never amount to anything."

In 2015, I was driving home when a car pulled out in front of me within fifty feet of an intersection. We collided. My car skidded off the road into someone's front yard. My car was completely totaled. Fortunately, I only had some mild soft tissue damage.

In my first job, in high school, I worked for a local grocery store. My manager would instruct me to go "front shelves" where you move products to the edge of the shelf so they look full and neat. He would stand behind me and watch me like a prison guard. It would make me so nervous. One day on the pickle aisle it happened. I dropped a jar of pickles and it exploded across the floor. My manager said, "I knew it. Now go clean it up," and walked away. It was some kind of psychological game for him.

I could go on and on. People are broken. Hurt people hurt people. Assaults are a reality of life. Victimization is bound to happen. While pain is real and healing can take time, it doesn't have to become an excuse. Life is what you make it.

Hopefully, you had healthy parents. If not, rise above them. Life is what you make it.

Hopefully, your bosses have helped you grow and flourish. If not, rise above them. Life is what you make it.

Hopefully your life has been a blessing to live. If not, rise above it. Life is what you and God make together!

As you will see in this book, you get to decide what kind of life you get to live. Perhaps you didn't get to decide what words you learned, but you get to decide what words you use.

Perhaps some very unfortunate things have happened to you. You get to decide to live bruised or blessed. Life is what you make it. You alone hold the keys in your hands. More specifically, you hold your own destiny on the tip of your tongue.

WHERE THERE'S A WILL THERE'S A WAY

I've now traveled to India over fifty times. I remember the first time I went to India; it was in a season of life when I didn't have the money to go. Our three children were nine, seven, and five, and I was unemployed. I went to church one Sunday, where a man stood up and shared about going to India, and I sensed God saying, "You're to go." I responded, "You provide, and I'll go." And that's exactly what He did. It changed the trajectory of my life forever.

At the time, I didn't realize it, but God's ONE word for me was: GO. The word GO has momentum. As I activated the word GO with my faith in God, something miraculous happened. Unfortunately, I know far too many people who have said "no" when God said GO. They didn't activate the momentum and haven't seen the miracles that only come when we GO.

It is important to inject the will of God into, "Where there's a will there's a way."

I experienced the call into vocational ministry during my senior year in high school. I went from begging my mom to let me drop out of school to enrolling for four years of college to prepare for ministry. My parents didn't make enough to help me pay for college, and they made too much for me to qualify for financial aid. I had no opportunity to take out loans. Fortunately, student loans were not very popular then.

Neither of my parents ever graduated with a four-year degree program. It was a miracle that I went to college. It was also a choice.

I worked multiple jobs to get myself through college, including being a personal care assistant to a quadriplegic veteran who was also enrolled. The U.S Department of Veterans Affairs paid me to bathe him, clothe him, and take care of him so he could attend school. This helped pay for my tuition, room, and board.

I graduated from college with only $5,000 debt that was forgiven a few years later.

"Where there's a will there's a way" goes hand-in-hand with "Life is what you make it."

HEAR IT AND CLAIM IT

I'm talking about hand-in-hand with God. I'm not talking about what some people refer to as "name it and claim it" Christianity. That's where we say we want a new luxury car and begin claiming God wants us to have a new luxury car. There is nothing wrong with a luxury car. The problem is bossing God around instead of surrendering our life completely over to Him and His will, regardless of material possessions.

I'm talking about "hear it and obey it." Instead of "name it and claim it" I'm talking about "hear it and claim it." There is a big difference between the two.

People who criticize name-it-and-claim-it practices oppose the "name it," not the "claim it." Name it suggests we dictate to God what we want. That's dangerous, especially if something is named that is questionable to align with the whole Word of God. Some people have claimed God wants them to have a younger spouse or even multiple spouses. These are contrary to God's Word.

On the other hand, to name and claim salvation for the lost aligns with Scripture. To name and claim a beach house for your family is inconsistent with scripture. There's nothing wrong with owning a beach house. The concern is bossing God around.

That is very different from hearing God speak a word and claiming that word.

THE POINT IS INTIMACY

Listen to God's desire for intimacy with you...

John 15:7 (ESV) says, "If you abide in me, and my words abide in you, ask whatever you wish, and it will be done for you."

Matthew 21:22 (NLT) says, "You can pray for anything, and if you have faith, you will receive it."

"All Scripture is God-breathed and is useful for teaching, rebuking, correcting, and training in righteousness, so that the servant of God may be thoroughly equipped for every good work," 2 Timothy 3:16–17 (NIV).

God's character never changes (Hebrews 13:8); He will continue to honor His covenant promises, dealing with His people in patience and faithfulness, even as we fall short time and time again.

THE PROMISE IS PRESENCE

God never promised the absence of problems. He promises to be present with us in the midst of problems. The whole point is His presence:

2 Timothy 3:12 (NLT), "Yes, and everyone who wants to live a godly life in Christ Jesus will suffer persecution."

John 16:33 (NLT), "I have told you all this so that you may have peace in me. Here on earth you will have many trials and sorrows. But take heart, because I have overcome the world."

1 Peter 4:12-13 (NLT), "Dear friends, don't be surprised at the fiery trials you are going through, as if something strange were happening to you. Instead, be very glad—for these trials make you partners with Christ in his suffering, so that you will have the wonderful joy of seeing his glory when it is revealed to all the world."

Jesus promises He will be with us in the midst of trials:

John 14:16-17 (NLT), "And I will ask the Father, and he will give you another Advocate, who will never leave you. He is the Holy Spirit, who leads into all truth. The world cannot receive him, because it isn't looking for him and doesn't recognize him. But you know him, because he lives with you now and later will be in you."

Hebrews 13:5 (NLT), "Don't love money; be satisfied with what you have. For God has said, 'I will never fail you. I will never abandon you.'"

2 Corinthians 1:20 (NLT), "For all of God's promises have been fulfilled in Christ with a resounding "Yes!" And through Christ, our "Amen" (which means "Yes") ascends to God for his glory."

Psalm 145:13 (NLT), "For your kingdom is an everlasting kingdom. You rule throughout all generations. The Lord always keeps his promises; he is gracious in all he does."

Sometimes we abandon God's promises because of problems. It's because of problems that we need to hold onto God's promises—ONE word at a time.

The only reason there is light in Genesis 1:3 is because God said, "Let there be light," and there was light. Darkness is a huge problem! Light is a miraculous provision from God. With ONE word God transformed the darkness.

What's Your Word? begins by asking God that very question: what's your word? Then, activating the word God speaks.

The Bible warns us, ". . . you have not because you ask not. And when you ask you don't ask God," (James 4:2).

Once you have heard God speak the word "college" over your life, you decide whether or not to go to college. God created the word college with momentum. When we engage, impulse, and activate God's word, college, He works miracles in our lives.

Once God has spoken "Olympics," you decide whether or not you'll compete in the Olympics. Because of the fall, you have to choose.

Once God has spoken "marriage," you decide whether or not to marry. You have to choose.

Once God says "now choose life," the decisions you make determine the quality of your life. You, not others, decide if you'll live rich or poor. Your choices will determine your income, investments, and returns. Some of the richest people I know have very little material wealth yet they are more wealthy in relationships and joy than we can imagine. You have to choose.

I want you to know that you can choose life! Don't allow the devil, yourself, or anyone to talk you out of living. Choose life. Live!
You have to choose. Your answer can be only ONE word.

What's Your Word?

You can choose your path ONE word at a time.

In the next chapter we'll begin to see, in ONE single word, why you need to choose life.

At the end of each chapter, I'll be inviting you to take five minutes to (1) Receive, (2) Respond, and (3) Repeat. Writing out your thoughts is a powerful way to engage in what God is saying to you.

"And the Holy Spirit also testifies that this is so. For he says, 'This is the new covenant I will make with my people, says the Lord: I will put my WORD in their hearts, and I will write it on their minds.'"

- Hebrews 10:15-17 (NLT)

1. **RECEIVE:** What is God revealing to you?

2. **RESPOND:** What will you do differently as a result of what God is giving you?

3. **REPEAT:** Who can you share with about this chapter?

CHAPTER 2

Now listen! Today I am giving you a choice between life and
death, between prosperity and disaster.

- Deuteronomy 30:15 (NLT)

Not only does God give us ONE word, "life," and plead with us to
choose life, He also tells us why: Because life leads to prosperity and
death leads to DISASTER. The purpose of this chapter is not just to
connect life to prosperity and death to DISASTER, but to begin helping
you see the power and momentum that words have. In the next chapter
we will do a deep dive into prosperity. First, in this chapter, I want to
point out the all too common realities of DISASTER.

CONTRADICTION

To expect that death apart from God would not be a disaster.

Unfortunately, we are bombarded with the realities of DISASTER all around us. Here's one example:

THREE DEAD AFTER SNOW FIGHT

January 5, 2021, was the snowiest day of the year in Scranton, Pennsylvania. The area received twenty-four inches of snow in one day. That morning before 9:00 a.m., neighbors say James and Lisa Goy shoved their snow onto Jeffrey Spaide's property. These two neighbors had been involved in a long-standing neighborhood feud. Jeffrey came out and asked James and Lisa to stop. They hurled insults at each other. James is seen throwing a tool at Jeffrey and raising his fist at Jeffrey. Neighbors heard both parties calling each other names.

Jeffrey went into his house, took a pistol, returned, and shot James and Lisa. Jeffrey goes back into his house, takes a rifle, returns and shoots James and Lisa again. When the police arrive they find James and Lisa lying dead in the snowy street. As police are going to Jeffrey's home to question him they hear a gunshot blast as Jeffrey takes his own life from a self-inflicted gunshot wound. [2]

The conflict all started with disrespectful attitudes and words. The two parties exchanged words long before shots were fired ending in three deaths.

We see it every day. Words result in DISASTER.

A MENTAL HEALTH CRISIS

Statistics show that murder-suicide is a growing trend. [3] In 2019, there were two and a half more suicides than homicides. [4] Globally, around 800,000 people die from suicide every year. That's one person every 40 seconds. [5]

More people die as a result of suicide than HIV, malaria, breast cancer, war or homicide. [6]

2020 was the deadliest year of gun violence in two decades. 2021 was worse! [7]

There are 11 murder-suicides in the US each week. Research shows suicides are contagious. People contemplating suicide are more likely to murder. [8]

As with James, Lisa, and Jeffrey, most conflicts resulting in deaths start with words. Long before guns are drawn words are hurled.

Let's follow this path...

God gives us ONE single word to choose:

1. Life

or

2. Death

We must choose ONE.

He pleads with us to choose life and tells us why. Because life leads to prosperity but death leads to DISASTER.

I hope you will accept that ONE word, death, leads to DISASTER.

WORDS ARE POWERFUL

You and I both know that someone could go into a crowded market, shout ONE word, and all hell would break loose. No crowd of people wants to hear:

- Fire
- Gun
- Bomb
- Robbery
- Hijack
- Hostage

I could go into any intersection and shout ONE word that invokes a road rage incident that gets me killed.

You could go into certain communities where you live and shout one word that is considered derogatory to that community and we would be conducting your funeral as a result.

Words are powerful. In Chapter Four we will see that God created words with momentum.

The reality is ONE single word can bring DISASTER. We see this every day. It is all too common. Allow me to address three other DISASTERS:

1. Putting words in God's mouth is a DISASTER.
2. Blocking words out of God's mouth is a DISASTER.
3. Hearing but not doing God's word is a DISASTER.

PUTTING WORDS IN GOD'S MOUTH

No doubt you've probably heard concerns about the "prosperity gospel." In a nutshell, the concern is that some people put words in God's mouth. They say, "God wants me to be a millionaire" and "God wants me to buy a private jet" or "God wants me to have a house on a Caribbean island." They practice the "name it and claim it" theology I mentioned earlier. They believe that whatever you name, claim, and believe by faith, you will receive.

The concern is whether we're bossing God around or surrendering to Him as the Lord of our lives.

There are huge disputes on both sides over the accuracy of interpretation of God's Word. Both sides accuse the other side of interpreting God's Word incorrectly. It is amazing how much time and energy is invested in disproving either side.

One of the reasons God had me write, *Get to the Point*, is to plead with us to just get to the point. God's whole point is us in His presence and His presence in us. The whole point of God's presence is intimacy.

No matter what side you're on, either side needs to be careful not to put words in God's mouth. We should be slow to say, "God says 'Yes'" or "God says 'No'" and be fast to say, "Pursue intimacy with God and you'll have no confusion whether or not God is saying yes or no."

Putting words in God's mouth is a DISASTER. Emphasizing disputes with man over intimacy with God is a DISASTER.

BLOCKING WORDS OUT OF GOD'S MOUTH

What is just as disastrous is our response to the concerns of the prosperity gospel. I've done this myself. For the longest time I shied away from God's promises in the bible afraid to claim anything for myself.

You don't have to convince me that I don't deserve God's promises. Under the influence of fear of the prosperity gospel I would celebrate God's goodness to others, but silently whisper, "that's not for me."

Another disastrous dispute occurs over claiming God's promises. A lot of time and energy is invested telling people they can't claim a promise God made to someone in the bible for themselves.

For example, millions of Christians have quoted Jeremiah 29:11 (NLT) for themselves, "For I know the plans I have for you," says the Lord. "They are plans for good and not for DISASTER, to give you a future and a hope." And throughout human history many devout preachers and theologians have warned that to do so is to take God's word out of context.

Many Christians say God's promise to Abraham is only for Abraham and not for future generations and certainly not for you or me.

I want to ask us—which would be better:

1. All of us claiming God's promises of prosperity and some of us being wrong about pursuing material possessions over intimacy with God?

   or

2. None of us claiming God's promises of prosperity because some of us might pursue material possessions over intimacy with God?

Paranoia over the prosperity gospel is exactly where the enemy wants us. As far as he is concerned, keep disputing! Keep telling people what they can't claim from God or what they can't expect God to do.

The response is to read the Bible as being written about others and for others, and not for any practical word for yourself. That's a DISASTER! That's blocking words out of God's mouth.

When someone says they were spending time with God and the Holy Spirit took them to Abraham's promise and said, "I'm going to bless you and make you a blessing, too," we should never block those words out of God's mouth.

What people who dispute the act of claiming Abraham's promise for yourself would say is, "You're not Abraham."

I've heard multiple people claim that the Holy Spirit told them, "Just as I blessed Abraham and told him I will make him a blessing, I'm going to bless you and make you a blessing, too." I've never heard anyone say, "God told me I am Abraham."

When we start cutting out parts of God's Word, thinking they do not apply to us, where do we stop cutting? Jesus didn't literally say to any of us, "Come to me and I will give you rest," so are you and I allowed to come to Jesus or not?

Should the Holy Spirit have freedom to speak any and all passages of the Bible over us? Yes, He should!

Could we get into trouble if we pick and choose what passages of Scripture apply to us? Yes, we could.

Once again, the need is intimacy with God. The need is not to tell each other what the Holy Spirit can and can't say. Could someone misuse this? Of course they could. What's worse? A few people using verses with entitlement or none of us claiming the promises of God for ourselves?

Blocking words out of God's mouth is a DISASTER.

Another way we block words out of God's mouth is to say God doesn't speak today. Believe it or not, some people dispute whether God speaks today.

As a father and grandfather, Matthew 7:11 (NLT) teaches me a lot about God: "So if you sinful people know how to give good gifts to your children, how much more will your heavenly Father give good gifts to those who ask him."

Can you imagine a good father never speaking to his children? All the expensive gifts in the world would be of little value if the father refused to speak even one single word over his children. Imagine the child never hearing the word "love." Never hearing the father say, "I am here."

I often put our 2-year-old granddaughter to bed at night. Sometimes she requests I lie down with her while she is falling asleep. Eventually her giggles and chattering will transition to deep breathing once she falls asleep. Sometimes I try to leave her room too soon and she will ask, "Poppy?" I will say, "I'm here. Goodnight."

She will roll over and go back to sleep.

According to Matthew 7:11, if I'm willing to say, "I'm here," to my granddaughter how much more willing is God to say, "I'm here," to me? The whole point of the Bible is you in God's presence and God's presence in you. Could you imagine being summoned into someone's presence who would never speak to you? The whole point of God's presence is intimacy. How is intimacy possible without communication?

Later in the book we will survey the words Jesus commonly used. One of the most commonly used words of Jesus is the word "hear." Actually, the Bible is filled with calls for you and me to hear. Why would God invite us to hear if He is not willing to speak today?

In addition, as we are able to see, the Bible is also filled with instructions for us to obey God's Word. Considering Matthew 7:11, how cruel would it be for a father to expect obedience but be unwilling to speak? Can you imagine someone expecting you to obey, but then never giving you a single instruction?

Matthew 7:11 assures us our good loving heavenly Father speaks today.

Blocking words out of God's mouth is a DISASTER.

HEARING BUT NOT DOING GOD'S WORD

Many people know God's Word. The Bible says that Satan and his demons know God's Word and tremble in fear (James 2:19).

We love to quote Jesus in John 8:32 (NLT), "And you will know the truth, and the truth will set you free." But we fail to apply John 8:31 (NLT), "Jesus said to the people who believed in him, You are truly my disciples if you remain faithful to my teachings."

Knowing and doing are two different things.

The Bible has a lot to say about obeying God's Word:

"If you love me, obey my commandments," John 14:15 (NLT).

"Jesus replied, "But even more blessed are all who hear the word of God and put it into practice," Luke 11:28 (NLT).

"Not everyone who calls out to me, 'Lord! Lord!' will enter the Kingdom of Heaven. Only those who actually do the will of my Father in heaven will enter. On judgment day many will say to me, 'Lord! Lord! We prophesied in your name and cast out demons in your name and performed many miracles in your name.' But I will reply, 'I never knew you. Get away from me, you who break God's laws,'" Matthew 7:21-23 (NLT).

"But don't just listen to God's word. You must do what it says. Otherwise, you are only fooling yourselves," James 1:22 (NLT).

To know is to hear, but only when we take action on what we know and hear do we obey. The Bible is clear that knowing the Word isn't the point. We are to obey.

Hearing but not doing God's Word is a DISASTER.

YOU CAN SEE IT

In Genesis 1, God saw everything he said. God said, "Let there be Light", and there was light. In Deuteronomy 30:15 God said death leads to DISASTER and he saw DISASTER.

When the collision of words results in murder and suicide, that's DISASTER. God establishes this truth:

> *Now listen! Today I am giving you a choice between life and death, between prosperity and disaster.*
> *- Deuteronomy 30:15 (NLT)*

God says, "death leads to DISASTER." You can see it.

You can also see the opposite is true. God says "Life leads to prosperity." You can see it.

The enemy is very sneaky and crafty to only show us one half of this truth. Every day we see how ONE word can result in DISASTER, but that is not all God said.

God also says "Life leads to prosperity."

Think about it, how often do you hear that ONE single word can bring prosperity? The devil has no problem showing you how a single word can bring DISASTER, but he hides from all of us the reality that ONE single word can bring prosperity. We will unpack prosperity in the next chapter. Before we do, though, I need to assure you that:

1. You can see it.
2. See what you say.

In Genesis 1 what did God see? He saw all that He said. God said, "Let there be light," and there was light. God saw all that He said.

SEE WHAT YOU SAY

What's your word? It is a matter of life and death.

1. If we say words of death, we will see DISASTER.
2. If we say words of life, we will see prosperity.

God has given us two words:

1. Life

or

2. Death

These words lead to two opposite paths:

1. Prosperity

or

2. Disaster

As you can see, one word can result in DISASTER, then you can also see that in the same way one word can result in prosperity. Not because you and I say so, but because God says so.

The path is yours.

What's Your Word?

You choose your path one word at a time.

The word death is a path that leads to DISASTER.

In the next chapter we will take a deep dive into PROSPERITY.

*"I have hidden your **WORD** in my heart, that I might not sin against you."*

- Psalm 119:11 (NLT)

1. **RECEIVE:** What is God revealing to you?

2. **RESPOND:** What will you do differently as a result of what God is giving you?

3. **REPEAT:** Who can you share with about this chapter?

CHAPTER 3

Now listen! Today I am giving you a choice between life and death, between prosperity and disaster.

- Deuteronomy 30:15 (NLT)

God set this in motion.

Death leads to a path of DISASTER. Life leads to a path of PROSPERITY.

The word you choose determines your path. You see what you say.

I don't know about you, but I am sick of having DISASTER rubbed in my face. I want to see PROSPERITY.

Unfortunately, even as a small child we are quickly confronted with DISASTER. Actually, it's shameful. So much innocence is lost because of ONE single word: DISASTER.

What's worse is that we know so little about PROSPERITY.

That is about to change!

John 10:10 says that the enemy of God, Satan, the devil comes as a thief to steal and kill and destroy. That's DISASTER.

John 10:10 also says Jesus' purpose is to give us a rich and satisfying life. That's PROSPERITY.

For too long Satan has blinded the minds of people to God's "why" for life. Just as death leads to DISASTER, God makes it clear that life leads to PROSPERITY.

CONTRADICTION

To deny God's promise of PROSPERITY over your life and not expect His prosperity is a contradiction to God's Word.

WHY CHOOSE LIFE? ANSWER: PROSPERITY

For the longest time I lived fully alive without any hope of PROSPERITY. I grew up poor. My parents never held a passport. I never hoped to fly over a million miles and travel to India fifty-one times. I never hoped of living on a budget, avoiding debt, having high quality relationships, saving and investing, or being outrageously generous. The word PROSPERITY was not even in my vocabulary.

I know from personal experience few things are more miserable than being alive and not knowing why. Too many people today are alive and don't know why. They are miserable. They have a heartbeat but no reason to live. Thousands of years ago God said:

> *Now listen! Today I am giving you a choice between life and death, between prosperity and disaster.*
> - *Deuteronomy 30:15 (NLT)*

God has said choose life because it results in PROSPERITY. But, when you're bombarded day in and day out with DISASTER you get weary about continuing to live.

In recent years we've been bombarded with a global pandemic from Covid-19. We've watched millions of people die, lose their jobs, and suffer. At the same time there've been the brutal murders of black lives by white police officers. There has been an uptick in extreme natural disasters including wildfires, floods, and tornadoes. And, if that is not enough, there's been a constant stream of international wars and rumors of wars. DISASTER is all around us. To make matters worse, all of these DISASTERS are unprovoked.

Yet none of these DISASTERS erases the other half of Deuteronomy 30:15. God has spoken. He has said life leads to PROSPERITY.

God never said, "Choose life for no reason at all." He says, "Choose life. It results in a path of PROSPERITY." Let's take a deeper dive into what God says about PROSPERITY.

Allow God to speak to you through His Word…

GOD'S PROMISE OF PROSPERITY

God has promised to prosper you:

Psalm 1:1-3 (NLT) says, "Oh, the joys of those who do not follow the advice of the wicked, or stand around with sinners, or join in with mockers. But they delight in the law (word) of the Lord, meditating on it day and night. They are like trees planted along the riverbank, bearing fruit each season. Their leaves never wither, and they PROSPER in all they do."

The context is a life saturated with the presence of God.

Can God be trusted? Is He who He says He is? Will He do what He says He will do? The answer is yes to all three questions. If so, then we need to hear and accept that Almighty God has promised to prosper us.

Proverbs 16:3 (NLT) says, "Commit your actions to the Lord, and your plans will succeed."

Did you see the word: maybe? No. Maybe is not there. It's not, "your plans will maybe succeed." It clearly says, "your plans will succeed." That's PROSPERITY. But it comes with a choice. It says, "Commit your actions to the Lord, and your plans will succeed." You have to choose.

Committing your actions to the Lord involves asking God to identify your actions. Do you go left or do you go right? This requires intimacy with God. That's God's whole point! The word "commit" has momentum. When you impulse it through obedience, then God releases his miracles as a result. Because of the fall you have to choose.

Jeremiah 29:11 (NIV) says, "For I know the plans I have for you," declares the Lord, "plans to PROSPER you and not to harm you, plans to give you hope and a future."

The English word PROSPERITY originates from the Hebrew word shalom. (9) Normally this word is translated as "peace." It is an indication of the absence of war and of economic success. Our English word PROSPERITY has come to describe economic well-being, with some implication of happiness, fulfillment, and satisfaction. But for shalom the primary meaning is being in good relationships with God and others, with some implication of welfare.

God wants more for us. God's more will always be more of Himself or more for Himself.

Often PROSPERITY gets a bad rap because it is associated only with material possessions and comfort. Those are actually only small elements of PROSPERITY.

We are never more prosperous than when we are in God's presence. God's greatest gift is Himself, not some material possession.

Most business owners go into business to make a profit. That's not a bad reason for business, but PROSPERITY is so much more than profit. God says He has a plan to PROSPER you, not just to give you a profit. Why settle for only a small portion (profit) when God has promised a much larger provision (PROSPERITY)?

PROSPERITY is the presence of God. It includes the gifts of God that money can't buy. You can't take your profit and go buy peace. You can't buy significance, security, or acceptance. You can't buy the fruits of the Spirit. Galatians 5:22-23 (NLT) says, "But the Holy Spirit produces this kind of fruit in our lives: love, joy, peace, patience, kindness, goodness, faithfulness, gentleness, and self-control. There is no law against these things!" All these things that money can't buy only come through a living relationship with God through Jesus Christ.

We get into trouble when we try to derive these gifts apart from God.

Life results in PROSPERITY. God doesn't say life might or hopefully will result in PROSPERITY. He says: "I am giving you a choice between life and death, between PROSPERITY and disaster." - Deuteronomy 30:15 (NLT)

LIFE RESULTS IN PROSPERITY

In order to fully grasp PROSPERITY, we need to fully understand life. God is not just talking about a beating heart. The heart is already beating. The implication is not physical life, but spiritual life.

When Adam and Eve rebelled against God, they didn't die physically. Instead, they lost their connection with the presence of God.

When God offers us His gift of eternal life, He is not giving us a product in a box or a certificate of life. He is giving us his very own life. He is eternal. He is what makes life eternal life. Jesus said, "I am the way, the truth, and the life. No one can come to the Father except through me." - John 14:6 (NLT)

God's gift of life is Himself through His Holy Spirit. When God says choose life, it leads to PROSPERITY, He is literally saying, "Choose Jesus, seek my presence, and you'll have everything you need" (Matthew 6:33).

PROSPERITY is a promise of God. The foundation is life. ONE word. Life. To God, this is specifically a life consecrated unto God.

Think about it. Your heart is beating with no choice of your own. God used your mother and father to give you life. You had no choice in it. Your choice is what you will do with this life. Will you live or will you die? Will you surrender your life over to God? Will you hear Him speak to you:

Now listen! Today I am giving you a choice between life and death, between prosperity and disaster.

- Deuteronomy 30:15 (NLT)

HOW DO WE CHOOSE TO LIVE?

Look at John 3 and see where Nicodemus asked Jesus this question:

There was a man named Nicodemus, a Jewish religious leader who was a Pharisee. After dark one evening, he came to speak with Jesus. "Rabbi," he said, "we all know that God has sent you to teach us. Your miraculous signs are evidence that God is with you."

Jesus replied, "I tell you the truth, unless you are born again, you cannot see the Kingdom of God."

"What do you mean?" exclaimed Nicodemus. "How can an old man go back into his mother's womb and be born again?"

Jesus replied, "I assure you, no one can enter the Kingdom of God without being born of water and the Spirit. Humans can reproduce only human life, but the Holy Spirit gives birth to spiritual life. So don't be surprised when I say, 'You must be born again.' The wind blows wherever it wants. Just as you can hear the wind but can't tell where it comes from or where it is

going, so you can't explain how people are born of the Spirit."
- John 3:1-8 (NLT)

Have you ever been born again? Call it conversion, commitment, repentance, or being saved, but has it happened to you? Have you acted on God's Word?

If so, 2 Corinthians 5:17 (NLT) says, ". . . anyone who belongs to Christ has become a new person. The old life is gone; a new life has begun!" That's life. This life leads to PROSPERITY.

1 Corinthians 3:16 (CEV) says that "you are God's temple and his Spirit lives in you." Does God the Holy Spirit live in you? That's true life. Not just a beating heart, but the Spirit of Jesus living inside of you through the Holy Spirit.

You can't spend meaningful time with Jesus without being prospered by Him. To be alive in Christ is to be prospered by God. That's PROSPERITY.

God's message has been consistent all throughout Scripture.

As King David was dying in 1 Kings 2:3 (NLT) he told his son Solomon: "Observe the requirements of the Lord your God, and follow all his ways. Keep the decrees, commands, regulations, and laws written in the Law of Moses so that you will be successful in all you do and wherever you go." The NIV says, "Do this so that you may prosper in all you do and wherever you go."

God has promised that as we pursue His presence and seek to live according to His ways that He will add in everything we need (Matthew 6:33). That's PROSPERITY!

In Genesis 39:2-6 (NLT) we see an example of PROSPERITY:

> *The Lord was with Joseph, so he succeeded in everything he did as he served in the home of his Egyptian master. Potiphar noticed this and realized that the Lord was with Joseph, giving him success in everything he did. This pleased Potiphar, so he soon made Joseph his personal attendant. He put him in charge of his entire household and everything he owned. From the day Joseph was put in charge of his master's household and property, the Lord began to bless Potiphar's household for Joseph's sake. All his household affairs ran smoothly, and his crops and livestock flourished. So Potiphar gave Joseph complete administrative responsibility over everything he owned.*

True Biblical PROSPERITY comes when we are in a living, dynamic relationship with God. When we are living moment by moment in His presence. When we are seeking to hear and obey His voice. If we look at the Bible as a whole, not just pieces here and there, we see God constantly calling His people into an intimate relationship with Himself.

GOD'S SOURCE OF PROSPERITY

"Trusting the LORD leads to PROSPERITY."

- Proverbs 28:25 (NLT)

God's presence is the source of eternal life. It is also the source of PROSPERITY. God can't give you one without the other. Deuteronomy says, "life and PROSPERITY" (Deuteronomy 30:15).

There is only one source for PROSPERITY and that is Almighty God. PROSPERITY does NOT come from our business or profits. God can use these, but the source is always God. James 1:6 (NLT) says, "But when you ask him, be sure that your faith is in God alone."

GOD'S WAY OF PROSPERITY

The Bible teaches us that God's way of prospering us is by others first:

In Philippians 2:3 (NIV) we read, "Do nothing out of selfish ambition or vain conceit. Rather, in humility, value others above yourselves."

Philippians doesn't offer any exceptions. It clearly says, "Do NOTHING out of selfish ambition." This includes business, ministry, or acts of kindness.

We will unpack this in Chapter Nine. It is important to understand that God's purpose for your PROSPERITY is far bigger than you.

GOD'S PURPOSE FOR PROSPERITY

Remember what I said earlier about God's "more"? God's more is always more OF Himself or more FOR Himself. Now apply this to PROSPERITY. God's purpose of PROSPERITY is more OF Himself and more FOR Himself. God is not being stingy and selfish. God is about His glory. Not ours. In order for God to be God, He can't share His glory with anyone.

God is all about people! God loves people. In John 3:16 we read, "For God so loved the world that He GAVE Jesus." God's desire for your PROSPERITY is for it to bring more of Him into your life and into the lives of others.

Hopefully, this crash course on PROSPERITY has increased your expectations.

We know too well that ONE wrong word can lead to DISASTER. God wants you to understand that ONE right word can lead to PROSPERITY.

Ready to prosper?

For the longest time my answer was "no." I actually thought PROSPERITY was bad. I thought PROSPERITY caused greed and corruption. It could, but the God who promises PROSPERITY has also put boundaries in place to protect us from greed and corruption. We'll be discussing these.

EXPECT PROSPERITY

I have a critical point I need to make.

On a scale of 1 to 10 how much do you expect your life to result in PROSPERITY?

Circle One...

No PROSPERITY 1 2 3 4 5 6 7 8 9 10 PROSPERITY

When it comes to PROSPERITY, we treat God like a broken promise. It is easier to accept God's willingness to prosper others than it is to accept that God has promised to prosper me.

Look at this again:

> *Now listen! Today I am giving you a choice between life and death, between prosperity and disaster.*
>
> *- Deuteronomy 30:15 (NLT)*

If you have chosen life in Christ, you can and should expect PROSPERITY. There is a law that governs this, just like the laws of gravity, reproduction, and physics. Allow me to prove it to you in the next chapter.

CONFIRMATION

The word "life" is a path that leads to God's PROSPERITY.

What's Your Word?

"Your **WORD** *is a lamp to guide my feet*
and a light for my path."

- Psalm 119:105 (NLT)

1. **RECEIVE:** What is God revealing to you?

2. **RESPOND:** What will you do differently as a result of what God is giving you?

3. **REPEAT:** Who can you share with about this chapter?

CHAPTER 4

We think COLLISIONS are bad. Some are, but most COLLISIONS are good. Some COLLISIONS are accidents. Some are intentional. I want to show you that the laws that cause COLLISIONS to result in disaster can also cause COLLISIONS to result in prosperity.

We see both COLLISIONS of disaster and COLLISIONS of prosperity around us every day.

First, there are COLLISIONS of disaster: Planes, trains, and automobiles collide every day. Since 1945, in fact, the USA has had two times more plane crashes than any other country in the world. [10] And every two hours in the USA, a person or vehicle collides with a train. [11]

Every day, almost 3,700 people are killed globally as cars, buses, motorcycles, bicycles, trucks, or pedestrians collide. [12]

Odds are you have a:

- 1 in 250,000 chance of dying as a result of colliding with a meteorite. [13]
- 1 in 60,000 chance of dying in a tornado. [14]
- 1 in 30,000 chance of dying in a plane crash. [15]
- 1 in 27,000 chance of dying from a flood. [16]

These are all accidental COLLISIONS of disaster.

Remember what I said earlier about murder, suicide, and gun violence? You only have a one in 185 chance of dying from murder. [17] These deaths are no accident. And most started with words.

Nothing collides more than words!

COLLISIONS resulting only in disaster and not prosperity are a contraction to the laws of science that God set forth in creation.

WORDS

By age one we know approximately forty words. By age three we have learned 1,000 words. We know 5,000 words by age four. This jumps to 10,000 words by age five. By age 50 we have learned 20,000 - 35,000 words. [18]

The average person speaks 7,000 words a day, with some speaking way more than that. [19]

With over 7 billion people alive today, if each person averaged 7,000 words that would be 49,000,000,000,000 or 49 trillion words per day.

Nothing collides more than words.

Each day less than 10 percent of our words actually communicate something of value. Ninety percent of our words are filler words. TMI (too much information) is real, costly, and even deadly.

The average family has six arguments a day, forty-two arguments a week, and 182 arguments a month. [20]

Nothing collides more than words.

The COLLISION of words is the number one reason for murders. Words always collide long before weapons are drawn.

What makes this happen? If we can see into COLLISIONS of disaster then we can discover the force behind COLLISIONS of prosperity.

For too long words have been used to destroy. It's time we use our words for prosperity instead of disaster.

The truth is that words can be destructive, even deadly. Fortunately, the opposite is true: the right word can produce prosperity.

I can prove it!

COLLISION = MOMENTUM + IMPULSE

We find the proof in Newton's Law of Physics.

Newton's law says a COLLISION = Momentum + Impulse.

PHYSICS IN A NUTSHELL:

Momentum is an object's tendency to stay in motion. Momentum is always going to go somewhere. Momentum is always conserved. When two objects collide the total momentum before the COLLISION is the same as the total momentum after the COLLISION.

In a COLLISION, the impulse experienced by an object is always equal to the momentum change.

Impulse is an object's change in momentum. In physics terms, impulse tells you how much the momentum of an object will change when a force is applied for a certain amount of time. When playing table pool, the taps you apply are called impulses. Force and time determine impulse.

Newton's second law of motion: Force equals mass times acceleration. Acceleration equals change in velocity over time. Velocity is the rate or speed of change. Velocity is direction-aware. [21]

COLLISIONS are more destructive, with more force over fewer periods of time. COLLISIONS are safer, with less force over longer periods of time.

A COLLISION can be either elastic or inelastic. Elastic is bouncy. A white ball hits a red ball and the white ball stops. Inelastic COLLISION is what happens when objects stay and move together.

Whenever an object in motion comes into contact with another object, we can call this event a COLLISION.

Newton's Third Law of Motion: Every action has an equal and opposite reaction.

Every murder/suicide is a COLLISION. Words or something set things into motion. That's momentum. At some point there is an impulse that results in someone pulling the trigger or doing something that results in death. And it all started with words.

WORDS HAVE MOMENTUM

Consider this. In Genesis 1 we read that God created the heavens and the earth. We see that the earth was formless and dark. Then everything changed! In just the third verse of the Bible we read: "Then God said, 'Let there be light,' and there was light," Genesis 1:3 (NLT).

Everything changed when God spoke. God said, "Let there be light." God spoke ONE word: light. What happened? There was light. Light has momentum.

We see COLLISIONS today every time someone says, "Turn on the light." The word, light, has momentum. It is sitting there waiting for an impulse. An impulse occurs when someone flips the switch and turns on the light. The light didn't just become light. It is already light. It already has momentum. It has a purpose. It has meaning. It is awaiting an impulse. Every time we turn on a light it's a COLLISION. It is momentum + impulse.

The word light has momentum, but you have to impulse it for there to be light.

LIGHT

This is only ONE Word: light.

Light is good.

In John 8:12 (NLT), Jesus said, "I am the light of the world. If you follow me, you won't have to walk in darkness, because you will have the light that leads to life."

Then Jesus said, "You are the light of the world—like a city on a hilltop that cannot be hidden. No one lights a lamp and then puts it under a basket. Instead, a lamp is placed on a stand, where it gives light to everyone in the house. In the same way, let your good deeds shine out for all to see, so that everyone will praise your heavenly Father" - Matthew 5:14-16 (NLT).

And we read, "God is light, and there is no darkness in him at all. So we are lying if we say we have fellowship with God but go on living in spiritual darkness; we are not practicing the truth. But if we are living in the light, as God is in the light, then we have fellowship with each other, and the blood of Jesus, his Son, cleanses us from all sin" - 1 John 1:5-7 (NLT).

This is only a small sampling of the word light in the Bible. The word light is used 272 times in the Bible. All because God said, "Let there be light" and there was light.

God said "light," and there was light.

Light has momentum. COLLISIONS with light bring prosperity far more than disaster. The odds of being struck by lightning in a given year are around one in 500,000. Every day there are billions of COLLISIONS of prosperity involving light.

The word light has momentum.

The word death has momentum.

The word life has momentum.

I can take the word death which has momentum and add an impulse of a bottle of pills and have a disaster.

I can take the word death which has momentum and add an impulse of a semiautomatic weapon and have a disaster.

And in the same way, I can take the word life which has momentum and add an impulse of a vaccine against disease and have prosperity.

I can take the word life which has momentum and add an impulse of seeking God's presence and have prosperity.

All collisions are momentum + impulse. Words have momentum. One single word has momentum for disaster or prosperity.

Unfortunately, we don't have to look far to see how words cause disaster. We see this everywhere we turn. Let me show you, though, how words lead to prosperity.

Imagine Amazon without the word "Buy," Apple without the word "Smart," or Chick-fil-A without the word "Eat."

AMAZON'S WORD IS "BUY"

The word "buy" has momentum. It awaits an impulse. Amazon has capitalized on the word buy. Amazon offers billions of products. Their goal is not just shopping. They want customers to buy, not just shop. Amazon has invested millions of dollars into making it as easy as possible for customers to buy. Every product offers a "buy now" button. As soon as you buy one product you are offered the opportunity to "buy it again." Amazon's word is most definitely buy.

Amazon backs up their word with quality products and competitive prices. And Amazon often offers same day or next day delivery, as well. They have exploded the marketplace with their ability to get people to buy. Every time a customer hits the buy now button, they create an impulse. We even call it "impulse buying." It can be a bad thing, but the vast majority of the time the impulse to buy is healthy and normal. Nevertheless, it is still an impulse.

COLLISION = momentum + impulse.

Amazon = buy + buy now.

The word buy has momentum and awaits someone to impulse it by pressing the "buy now" button. Every civilization since the beginning of time has seen buying as a sign of prosperity.

Now Amazon is not perfect, but ideally everyone prospers every time someone hits the buy now button. Customers prosper. Amazon prospers. The environment prospers. Even their boxes smile.

APPLE'S WORD IS "SMART"

The word "smart" has momentum. Smart or wisdom is also a sign of prosperity. The world's agriculture that feeds the globe has benefited greatly from the word smart. Without all the smart advances, we'd all be starving right now.

Apple leads with the word smart. They create smart technology that makes their customers smart. While other companies focus on the look of their products, Apple has dominated the market with the word smart. Of course, style is also important to Apple. They are definitely known for their modern look, but their core value is in their smart products and how they make their users smarter too.

A COLLISION of prosperity happens every time a customer impulses Apple's word smart. Smart has momentum and when you impulse it, prosperity, not disaster, usually follows.

I'm not saying that people's IQs go up. I'm saying a person's quality of life goes up. Apple's mission is to provide products that allow people to work smarter instead of harder.

The point is, God created words to have momentum. While Apple is not a perfect company we can still learn a lot from their success at creating COLLISIONS of prosperity as people impulse their word smart. The same is true of Chick-fil-A.

CHICK-FIL-A'S WORD IS "EAT"

Chick-fil-A's slogan is, "Eat More Chicken".

Chick-fil-A has been very successful in getting people to eat.

The word eat has momentum. When impulsed it usually leads to prosperity. Actually, starvation is a sign of impoverishment. Starvation is an unfortunate disaster. All throughout human history, eating has been a sign of prosperity. It sustains life. It allows more opportunity. It provides a future. Stop eating long enough and the result is death.

When Chick-fil-A's word eat collides with an impulse, it results in prosperity. The customer prospers, Chick-fil-A prospers, farmers prosper——everyone prospers.

COLLISIONS OF PROSPERITY

COLLISIONS of prosperity are happening all around us every day. They don't make the news or get the attention that COLLISIONS of disaster receive.

I'm laying all this out to make a pivotal point:

COLLISIONS of prosperity can be harnessed! Therefore, you can choose a path of prosperity one word at a time.

Amazon isn't flippantly tossing the word buy out for no apparent reason. Apple isn't casual about their word smart. Chick-fil-A isn't randomly using the word eat.

There are many other great examples we could use. The point is that these words have momentum and they await a desired impulse. There is a very intentional strategy behind the use of each of these words.

There is a reason for these successes in business. This isn't just random magic at play. This is the very law of God at work. God creating words with momentum is as sure as His creations of the law of gravity, physics, and reproduction.

THE LAW OF REPRODUCTION

In Genesis Chapter One God establishes the law of reproduction:

> *Then God said, "Let the waters swarm with fish and other life. Let the skies be filled with birds of every kind." So God created great sea creatures and every living thing that scurries and swarms in the water, and every sort of bird—**each producing offspring of the same kind.***
>
> *And God saw that it was good. Then God blessed them, saying, "**Be fruitful and multiply.** Let the fish fill the seas, and let the birds multiply on the earth." - Genesis 1:20-22 (NLT)*

In Genesis 1:22-25, God did the same with animals and livestock. And in Genesis 1:26-28 (NLT), God did the same with humans:

> Then God said, "Let us make human beings in our image, to be like us. They will reign over the fish in the sea, the birds in the sky, the livestock, all the wild animals on the earth, and the small animals that scurry along the ground."

> So God created human beings in his own image.
> In the image of God he created them; male and female he created them.

> Then God blessed them and said, "**Be fruitful and multiply**. Fill the earth and govern it. Reign over the fish in the sea, the birds in the sky, and all the animals that scurry along the ground."

In Genesis 1:29-31 (NLT), God did the same with plants:

> Then God said, "Look! I have given you every seed-bearing plant throughout the earth and all the fruit trees for your food. And I have given every green plant as food for all the wild animals, the birds in the sky, and the small animals that scurry along the ground—everything that has life." And that is what happened.

> Then God looked over all he had made, and he saw that it was very good!

Here are the two laws of reproduction God established:

1. Same
2. Multiplication

These laws govern all reproduction.

SAME

Gorillas reproduce gorillas. Imagine if a gorilla gave birth to a dolphin or if an eagle gave birth to an elephant. Death would be imminent.

An apple seed produces more apples. Imagine if you planted tomato seeds but got thirty-six different plants, none of which were tomatoes. This would cause great disorder.

Fortunately, gorillas reproduce gorillas, dolphins reproduce dolphins, eagles reproduce eagles, and elephants reproduce elephants.

Thankfully, apple seeds reproduce apples and tomato seeds reproduce tomatoes.

God created the law of "same"—each reproduces its own kind.

The law of reproduction applies to all of creation.

Job 4:8 (NLT) says, "My experience shows that those who plant trouble and cultivate evil will harvest the same."

You'll want to appreciate this when it comes to words:

- Life produces life.
- Death produces death.
- Prosperity produces prosperity.
- Disaster produces disaster.

Whether you realize it or not, you are governed by the reproductive law of same—each reproduces its own kind. It is to your advantage to appreciate this law when it comes to the words you use. You choose your path by the words you use. You can't invest in the word death and experience life and prosperity.

CORRUPTION REPRODUCES MORE CORRUPTION

I've been leading mission trips to India for nearly twenty-five years. And I've been to India over fifty times taking 1,000 people with me on short-term mission trips. I love India. Unfortunately, like many other countries, India has a bad reputation for corruption. In order to find good paying jobs in India you have to pay bribes to get employment. Police with low salaries will stop and fine motorists for violations in order to generate more income for themselves. They don't issue formal tickets but instead tell drivers, "Give me $10 or I'll confiscate your scooter." Land purchases and construction projects require bribes, as well. Politicians promise road improvement for votes but then take funds meant for roads and make themselves and their friends rich. There is a great deal of corruption.

India is not alone. Corruption happens everywhere, and corruption is actually prosperity at the expense of others. My international travels have exposed me to the reality that:

1. Corruption produces corruption.
2. Prosperity produces prosperity.

It is the reproductive law of "same."

The only thing you will ever get from corruption is more corruption. Throughout human history any oppressor or dictator who got rich at the expense of others was found to be corrupt. Not one prospered, because corruption only produces more corruption. It's as sure as the law of gravity. Corrupt others and corruption will be ringing at your door.

It is just like, "Feed others and you will eat," prosper others and you will prosper. Employ others and you will have employment. Give good salaries to others and you'll have a good salary. Shelter others and you'll have shelter. Prosperity produces prosperity.

MULTIPLICATION

The second reproductive law is the law of "multiplication."

God created the fact that out of one could come many. The average gorilla mother has two offspring that survive. On average a dolphin mother can birth three dolphins in her lifetime. An eagle mother can lay twenty eggs in her lifetime. Only one in ten eagles survives until adulthood. One elephant mother can birth twelve baby elephants in her lifetime.

On average, women have two children during their lives. [22]

One tomato seed can produce ten to thirty pounds of tomatoes, or twenty to ninety tomatoes.

> *"Though you can easily count the seeds in an apple, it is*
> *impossible to count the apples in a seed."*
>
> *- unknown*

Each apple seed can produce one apple tree. The average apple tree produces about 300 apples in a growing season. Let's say that the average apple contains five apple seeds. So all things being equal, one apple tree will produce about 1,500 seeds per season. Those 1,500 seeds will potentially produce 450,000 apples, and another 2,250,000 seeds. It's impossible to count how many apples will be produced from just one apple seed. The amount is staggering and impossible to predict. [23]

God created the law of multiplication—out of one come many.

The law of reproduction applies to all of creation.

Genesis 26:12 (NLT) says, "When Isaac planted his crops that year, he harvested a hundred times more grain than he planted, for the Lord blessed him."

The law of reproduction is also known as sowing and reaping. It applies to all of creation, not just animals, plants, and humans.

In Galatians 6:7-10 (NLT), we read, "Don't be misled—you cannot mock the justice of God. You will always harvest what you plant. Those who live only to satisfy their own sinful nature will harvest decay and death from that sinful nature. But those who live to please the Spirit will harvest everlasting life from the Spirit. So let's not get tired of doing what is good. At just the right time we will reap a harvest of blessing if we don't give up. Therefore, whenever we have the opportunity, we should do good to everyone—especially to those in the family of faith."

GENEROSITY

Consider the word "generosity."

Same, multiplication, sowing and reaping don't apply only to good seeds, they also apply to good deeds. God encourages us to take advantage of this law and rewards us when we impulse the momentum of this word:

In 2 Corinthians 9:6-11 (NLT), we read,

> *"Remember this—a farmer who plants only a few seeds will get a small crop. But the one who plants generously will get a generous crop. You must each decide in your heart how much to give. And don't give reluctantly or in response to pressure. "For God loves a person who gives cheerfully." And God will*

generously provide all you need. Then you will always have
everything you need and plenty left over to share with others.
As the Scriptures say,

"They share freely and give generously to the poor.
Their good deeds will be remembered forever."

For God is the one who provides seed for the farmer and then
bread to eat. In the same way, he will provide and increase your
resources and then produce a great harvest of generosity in you.

Yes, you will be enriched in every way so that you can always be
generous. And when we take your gifts to those who need them,
they will thank God.

The word generosity is full of momentum from God. It activates:

1. Same
2. Multiplication

God pleads with us to sow generously, for it will reap a harvest of
generosity.

Generosity produces generosity.

In Luke 6:38 (ESV), Jesus says, "Give, and it will be given to you. Good
measure, pressed down, shaken together, running over, will be put into
your lap. For with the measure you use it will be measured back to you."

GOD MAKES THE SEED GROW

In 1 Corinthians 3:5-9 (NLT), we see:

> *After all, who is Apollos? Who is Paul? We are only God's servants through whom you believed the Good News. Each of us did the work the Lord gave us. I planted the seed in your hearts, and Apollos watered it, but it was God who made it grow. It's not important who does the planting, or who does the watering. What's important is that God makes the seed grow. The one who plants and the one who waters work together with the same purpose. And both will be rewarded for their own hard work. For we are both God's workers. And you are God's field. You are God's building.*

The multiplication comes from God not from you or me. We can only plant, but God is who makes the seeds grow. This isn't decided seed by seed today. This is decided in Genesis 1. It's the law of reproduction. Momentum is guaranteed by God. It's a law.

God created words with momentum. Words are awaiting an impulse. When we impulse the momentum in words we can choose our path one word at a time.

It is as sure as the law of gravity which says, "What goes up must come down." - Isaac Newton

HARVEST IS GUARANTEED

In Psalm 126:5-6 (NLT), we read,

> *"Those who plant in tears*
> *will harvest with shouts of joy.*
> *They weep as they go to plant their seed,*
> *but they sing as they return with the harvest."*

In John 4:34-38 (NLT), Jesus said,

> *"My nourishment comes from doing the will of God, who sent me, and from finishing his work. You know the saying, 'Four months between planting and harvest.' But I say, wake up and look around. The fields are already ripe for harvest. The harvesters are paid good wages, and the fruit they harvest is people brought to eternal life. What joy awaits both the planter and the harvester alike! You know the saying, 'One plants and another harvests.' And it's true. I sent you to harvest where you didn't plant; others had already done the work, and now you will get to gather the harvest."*

Jesus' audience understood farming. Jesus regularly used parables or earthly stories to reveal heavenly truth. He constantly interchanged eternal life, good deeds, and material things together. The law of reproduction is not reserved for just fruits' and vegetables' seeds, nor animals' and humans'. It governs all reproduction.

BABIES RESULT FROM COLLISIONS

We get beautiful babies as a result of God's law of reproduction. When men and women come together sexually the result can be a baby. This is an example of a good COLLISION. We would say a COLLISION of prosperity.

COLLISION = Momentum + Impulse

- Death produces a harvest of disaster.
- Life produces a harvest of prosperity.
- Disaster produces disaster.
- Corruption produces corruption.
- Prosperity produces prosperity.
- Generosity produces generosity.

MOMENTUM

The point is that God created words with momentum. Momentum is an object's tendency to stay in motion. In the following chapters I want to break down this momentum into five practical applications:

1. **VISION:** God created words to cast vision.
2. **VALUE:** God created words to instill value.
3. **WHY:** God created words to identify why.
4. **NOISE:** God created words to eliminate noise.
5. **EVERYONE:** God created words to prosper everyone.

As we will see, our individual word, the word God speaks over us, the word we prophesy over ourselves and others will:

1. Cast VISION
2. Instill VALUE
3. Identify WHY
4. Eliminate NOISE
5. Prosper EVERYONE

That's practical. That's momentum.

Remember, a COLLISION is momentum plus impulse.

IMPULSE

You have to choose whether or not you will impulse your word. To impulse is to activate.

ACTIVATE

When God says, "Let there be light," there was light. Today, when you turn on the lights you activate what was already created and waiting for you to activate. To impulse is to obey.

OBEY

When God says, "Love your neighbor as yourself," you have a choice whether or not you will obey. When you obey you reap the benefits of the word love. You activate the momentum in the word love. The word love is a powerful word, but its power is released as it is obeyed. Ignore the word love and you'll not experience it. To impulse is to do.

DO

Love is action. So is faith. Consider James 2:14-20 (NLT),

> *What good is it, dear brothers and sisters, if you say you have faith but don't show it by your actions? Can that kind of faith save anyone? Suppose you see a brother or sister who has no food or clothing, and you say, "Good-bye and have a good day; stay warm and eat well"—but then you don't give that person any food or clothing. What good does that do?*
>
> *So you see, faith by itself isn't enough. Unless it produces good deeds, it is dead and useless.*
>
> *Now someone may argue, "Some people have faith; others have good deeds." But I say, "How can you show me your faith if you don't have good deeds? I will show you my faith by my good deeds."*

You say you have faith, for you believe that there is one God.
Good for you! Even the demons believe this, and they tremble in
terror. How foolish! Can't you see that faith without good deeds
is useless?

To impulse God's word means to activate, obey, and do or take action on the momentum God places within the word.

God created words with momentum. The words you impulse
determine your path.

In the next chapter we will see how God created words with VISION.

Let me ask you . . .

What's your word?

*"For the **WORD** of God is alive and powerful. It is sharper than the sharpest two-edged sword, cutting between soul and spirit, between joint and marrow. It exposes our innermost thoughts and desires."*

- Hebrews 4:12 (NLT)

1. **RECEIVE:** What is God revealing to you?

2. **RESPOND:** What will you do differently as a result of what God is giving you?

3. **REPEAT:** Who can you share with about this chapter?

CHAPTER 5

In Genesis Chapter One, God created tomato seeds with the VISION of tomatoes. Each tomato seed carries the VISION of tomatoes. Every apple seed carries the VISION of apples. God also created words to carry VISION.

When we hear words, God hears VISION.

When we see words, God sees VISION.

When we speak words, God hears VISION.

If you don't already, then by the end of this chapter you will too!

This VISION inside individual words is waiting to be opened, activated, obeyed, and put into action.

Whether we have realized it or not, we have already been choosing our path one word at a time according to the words we impulse or activate.

Look at what God says about the power of VISION:

> *"When people do not accept divine guidance, they run wild.*
> *But whoever obeys the law (word) is joyful."*
> *- Proverbs 29:18 (NLT)*

The King James Version says, "Where there is no VISION, the people perish." They die.

VISION is divine guidance from God.

Notice the phrase, "But whoever obeys the law is joyful." Another way to say this is, "But whoever impulses the word is joyful." That's VISION.

Throughout the Bible, the word "law" is interchangeable with the word "word." Sometimes we think of obedience as an attempt to follow the rules.

I want you to see that impulsing or acting on the momentum in the words God has created is another way to understand obedience. If I ask someone to turn on the lights it is possible for them to follow my request and turn on the light without ever consciously committing to live in the light. There's a big difference.

God doesn't just want a bunch of rule followers for no point at all. God wants intimacy with us. God wants us to impulse His word for its intended purposes—for which he created it. God's VISION isn't just a life full of conformity to His rules, but it's our prosperity as a result of impulsing His Word.

As stated above, VISION is divine guidance from God. The ability to see God's VISION happens through an intimate relationship with God through Jesus Christ. God's gift to us is not a bunch of words, but Himself. God's Holy Spirit in us helps us to see the VISION that God has created words to carry.

VISION can be a matter of life or death.

It's a glorious cycle:

Life brings VISION.
VISION brings life.

We enter life as offspring of our parents. We have no choice in the matter. Eventually we have to determine where we are heading in life or what we want out of life. Remember where we started in Chapter One:

> *Now listen! Today I am giving you a choice between life and*
> *death, between prosperity and disaster.*
> *- Deuteronomy 30:15 (NLT)*

As God offers us this choice between life and death, He is also offering us a choice between two VISIONS. Will we choose prosperity or disaster?

What is your VISION for your life?

Is your life characterized by prosperity or disaster?

Every one of us has experienced some form of disaster, but you should see your life becoming more prosperous.

A life without the VISION of prosperity from God is a contradiction.

ONE VISION FOR DEATH

In Chapter Two we looked at disaster. The VISION of death is disaster. In the Bible, death is not just what happens when a heart stops beating. Ultimately, death is what happens when someone dies apart from God. God says this is a disaster.

Matthew 10:28 (NLT) says, "Don't be afraid of those who want to kill your body; they cannot touch your soul. Fear only God, who can destroy both soul and body in hell."

Dying and spending eternity apart from God in hell is a disaster. It's an eternal punishment that is 100 percent avoidable if we would just choose life through Jesus Christ.

Referring to those who die without a living relationship with Jesus, Matthew 25:46 (NLT) says, "And they will go away into eternal punishment, but the righteous will go into eternal life."

The Bible describes hell as a fiery lake of burning sulfur:

Revelation 21:8 (NLT) says, "But cowards, unbelievers, the corrupt, murderers, the immoral, those who practice witchcraft, idol worshipers, and all liars—their fate is in the fiery lake of burning sulfur. This is the second death."

By second death the Bible is distinguishing between physical death and spiritual death. Physical death is a reality of life. In Hebrews 9:27-28 (NLT), we read:

> And just as each person is destined to die once and after that comes judgment, so also Christ was offered once for all time as a sacrifice to take away the sins of many people. He will come again, not to deal with our sins, but to bring salvation to all who are eagerly waiting for him.

The VISION of life is prosperity in the presence of God for all eternity in heaven.

The VISION of death is disaster outside the presence of God for all eternity in hell.

Hell is miserable. Hell is a disaster.

That's the disaster God is referring to in Deuteronomy 30:15. Is that your VISION? Is that where you're headed? Is disaster your destiny? I hope not.

The choice is yours. You could choose death and disaster if you want. God is pleading with you to choose life and prosperity.

THE VISION OF LIFE IS PROSPERITY

Many people have beating hearts and are fully alive physically, but they have no VISION. Suicide happens when people see no reason to live. Murders happen when people choose to bestow death over life.

Without VISION, people die.

The opposite is also true.

With VISION, people live.

ONE VISION FOR LIFE

In Chapter Three we looked at prosperity. Now let's look at prosperity as the VISION for life.

God is offering you one VISION for life:

Now listen! Today I am giving you a choice between life and
death, between prosperity and disaster.

- Deuteronomy 30:15 (NLT)

God's one and only VISION for life is prosperity. He offers no plan B.

As we discussed in Chapter Three, we know so little about prosperity. I know from personal experience how miserable it is to be alive without any sense of purpose for your life. It is unfortunate for anyone to be alive and not have a VISION of God's prosperity for their life.

As soon as a baby is born God is asking:

Now listen! Today I am giving you a choice between life and
death, between prosperity and disaster.

- Deuteronomy 30:15 (NLT)

God is saying, "I have given you life for prosperity. Now choose life."

God's VISION for your life is prosperity. God's whole point for your life is you in His presence and His presence in you. We are never more prosperous than when we are in the presence of God.

When you ask God: What's your word over my life? His reply is prosperity. It isn't His only word, but it is a foundational word.

God's VISION could have been: profit, peace, survival, or comfort. God's one and only VISION for your life is prosperity.

It is not just profit. It is not just comfort. Prosperity is way bigger than just making a profit and living in comfort.

What's Your Word?

Is prosperity your VISION for your life?

If not it should be—right here, right now. Don't argue this out with God for the next ten years. Accept it today.

God said, "Let there be light" and there was light. The same God has said, "Now choose life and prosperity."

A VISION OF PROSPERITY

The word "life" has momentum. It is awaiting your choice. Life is not automatic. You have to choose to live. Let me repeat that: You have to choose it.

Life happens as a result of a COLLISION. This COLLISION doesn't end in disaster. It ends in prosperity. When we choose (impulse) life (momentum) the result is a collision of prosperity.

COLLISION (prosperity) = momentum (life) + impulse (activation).

This VISION isn't whatever life you can make apart from Jesus. This VISION is God's life in you through Jesus.

We can't come to God, ask for prosperity and then go live a life apart from God. It doesn't work like this. God is offering you life in Jesus, and when you choose this the VISION is prosperity.

Oftentimes we treat God as a "been there done that." We treat Him like a prayer we prayed ten years ago. We treat Him like someone we met earlier in our life instead of having a living relationship with Him today.

Choosing life is not a one-time choice, it is a continual choice. We don't just go turn on our lights one time and call it done. We continually turn on our lights. The same is true of choosing life. It's a daily choice. It leads to prosperity.

You choose your path one word at a time.

The consequence of the fall of Adam and Eve is that you now have to choose. If you don't choose life then you can miss God's whole VISION of prosperity for your life. The choice is yours. The word life has momentum whether you choose to impulse it or not.

CHOOSE LIFE

Accept God's VISION of prosperity over your life.

You are not here by accident. You are not here just to survive until you can finally die. God has so much more to offer you than just a meaningless existence.

If you have never taken Jesus solely for salvation before, right here, today, is why you should do so. When I was ten years old I prayed a prayer like this one:

> *Dear Lord Jesus, I know that I am a sinner, and I ask for Your forgiveness. I believe You died for my sins and rose from the dead. I turn from my sins and invite You to come into my heart and life. I choose to trust and follow You as my Lord and Savior. In Your Name. Amen.*

If you have never prayed this prayer before, I recommend you to pray it now and commit your life to God today. If so, hallelujah! Tell someone and let me know at kevin@kevinwhite.us. I pray God opens your eyes to His VISION for your life. Congratulations on making the best decision you will ever make!

Forgiveness of sin is only a small part of prosperity. It is what makes prosperity possible. God's whole point is you in His presence and His presence in You. I don't care if you are saved or not. That's not the point. Salvation is only a means to the point. Many people have never seen the point of salvation. They have never seen the reason to be forgiven of their sin, to have a personal relationship with God through Jesus Christ.

The reason for Jesus, forgiveness, and salvation is to fulfill God's VISION of prosperity over your life. It's the only way to choose life. If your VISION as a believer of God is to avoid hell and go to heaven, you're only seeing a small part of God's VISION of prosperity for your life. Prosperity isn't something that starts when you go to heaven. Prosperity begins the moment you choose life.

What's Your Word?

Show me your VISION and I'll show you your words. Show me your words and I'll show you your VISION. You choose your path one word at a time.

I regularly help people see the God-given vision for their life, business, or projects like books. I take them through an exercise of listing out all the words that describe their values. We add in words other people say about them. We put similar words into various groups. We talk through word after word until we narrow their words down to their top ten words, then their top five words, then their top three, and eventually arrive at their one word over their life, or their business, or book. This exercise has helped people illuminate specific words over their life.

One person saw how they help people discover their purpose. That's VISION. Their word was "purpose." Another person saw how they help people accelerate the growth of their companies. That's VISION. Their word was "accelerate." Another person's word was "beautiful." They are an artist and they create beautiful art. They make walls and homes beautiful. That's VISION. Each word declares VISION.

YOU CAN CHANGE YOUR VISION

VISION determines destiny. Where are you headed? How will your life end up? The me I see is the me I will be. If you see yourself as a victim, then you'll be a victim. If you see yourself as a victor in Christ, you'll have the victory.

I learned this the hard way. I used to struggle with poor self-esteem. I constantly felt like a failure no matter how successful I was. It was never enough. I always had to do more and work harder to measure up. I nearly killed myself and my marriage trying to do great things for God. Then some friends discipled me in my identity in Christ. I began to see and hear straight from Scripture how God saw me and what God said about me. The difference was night and day.

I was totally wrong in how I saw myself. It was a product of my past. As a follower of Jesus I had a choice. Either I could see myself outside of Christ or I could hear and accept what God was saying in his Word about me. I began practicing an exercise of renouncing lies I believed about myself and affirming truth from God's Word. For weeks I camped out on these scriptures about our identity in Christ:

Who I Am in Christ
By Dr. Neil Anderson

I am Significant:

- Matt 5:13-14 I am the salt and light of the earth.
- John 15:1-5 l am a branch of the true vine, a channel of His life.
- John 15:16 I have been chosen and appointed to bear fruit.
- Acts 1:8 I am a personal witness of Christ's.
- I Cor. 3:16 I am God's temple.

- 2 Cor. 5:17-21 I am a minister of reconciliation for God.

- 2 Cor. 6:1 I am God's co-worker.

- Eph. 2:6 I am seated with Christ in the heavenly realm.

- Eph. 2:10 I am God's workmanship.

- Eph. 3:12 I may approach God with freedom and confidence.

- Phil. 4:13 I can do all things through Christ who strengthens me.

I am Accepted:

- John 1:12 I am God's child.

- John 15:15 I am Christ's friend.

- Rom. 5:1 I have been justified.

- I Cor. 6:17 I am united with the Lord, and I am one spirit with Him.

- 1 Cor. 6:19-20 I have been bought with a price. I belong to God.

- I Cor. 12:27 I am a member of Christ's body.

- Eph.1:1 I am a saint.

- Eph. 1:5 I have been adopted as God's child.

- Eph. 2:18 I have direct access to God through the Holy Spirit.

- Col. 1:14 I have been redeemed and forgiven of all my sins.

- Col. 2:10 I am complete in Christ.

I am Secure:

- Rom. 8:1-2 I am free forever from condemnation.
- Rom. 8:28 I am assured that all things work together for good.
- Rom. 8:31-34 I am free from any condemning charges against me.
- Rom. 8:35-39 I cannot be separated from the love of God.
- 2 Cor. 1:21-22 I have been established, anointed, and sealed by God.
- Col. 3:3 I am hidden with Christ in God.
- Phil. 1:6 I am confident that the good work that God has begun in me will be perfected.
- Phil. 3:20 I am a citizen of heaven.
- 2 Tim. 1:7 I have not been given a spirit of fear but of power, love, and a sound mind.
- Heb. 4:16 I can find grace and mercy in time of need.
- I Jn. 5:18 I am born of God, and the evil one cannot touch me.

I began reading this out loud every day for several weeks. It was profound. Slowly my VISION began to change.

If you too struggle with fear, guilt, and rejection, I highly recommend you read this out loud every day. Remember, when God hears words, He hears VISION. I encourage you to read this out loud. It will empower you with a VISION for your life.

In Christ you are absolutely significant, secure, and accepted. The VISION of God's work IN you is foundational to the VISION of God's work THROUGH you.

Romans 12:2 says, ". . . let God transform you into a new person by changing the way you think." It's that simple, but the choice is up to you. Who controls your VISION? You, your past, or Almighty God? Let God speak His Word over you. Reject all other VISIONS for your life. And accept God's VISION.

WHAT SIZE IS YOUR VISION?

Why should God prosper you, your family, and your business? What's your VISION for others?

As we will see in Chapter Nine, the momentum God has placed into words is for everyone, not just you. And, not just me.

Most people go into business just to make money. The purpose of business is not profit. God only has one VISION for all of life and that is prosperity. God's VISION for your business is prosperity. As we've discussed, profit is only a small part of prosperity.

Matthew 16:26 (NKJV) says, "For what profit is it to a man if he gains the whole world, and loses his own soul?" Material possessions are only a small part of prosperity. God wants to include all the gifts and treasures that money can't buy.

2 Peter 1:5-7 (NLT) says, "In view of all this, make every effort to respond to God's promises. Supplement your faith with a generous provision of moral excellence, and moral excellence with knowledge, and knowledge with self-control, and self-control with patient endurance, and patient endurance with godliness, and godliness with brotherly affection, and brotherly affection with love for everyone."

Ask God, "What's your word over my life?" and he will include:

- excellence
- knowledge
- self-control
- endurance
- godliness
- affection
- love

This is what leads to peace, fulfillment, and satisfaction.

It's not that God is nonprofit. Actually, quite the contrary! God wants you to have more profit than you do. He also wants your purity. He wants the profit to be a blessing, not a curse. He wants your prosperity.

As a serial entrepreneur, I've helped to start hundreds of businesses, nonprofits, and churches. One thing I've learned from the nonprofit world is that money follows VISION. A charity must effectively cast VISION if it expects to have any donations. The same is true in business. Without VISION, people die. Without VISION, businesses die. The lack of VISION is what holds most businesses back. Often, their VISION is too small. They want profit without prosperity. There is a huge difference.

- Amazon's VISION is buy.
- Apple's VISION is smart.
- Chick-fil-A's VISION is eat.

They have made lots of profit as a result of these words.

- BUY has momentum and leads to prosperity.
- SMART has momentum and leads to prosperity.
- EAT has momentum and leads to prosperity.

Perhaps you can point to imperfections in Amazon, Apple, and Chick-fil-A. Fortunately, imperfection doesn't dismiss principle. I'm not trying to convince you of their perfection. Rather, I am inviting you to see the absolute principles in God's Word. That's VISION. I encourage you to take the principles I'm sharing and apply them to your life and business.

How do you measure success for your life: profit or prosperity? The answer should be prosperity.

I encourage you to understand and accept that God's VISION for your life is prosperity. This is God's only VISION for every life.

> *Now listen! Today I am giving you a choice between life and*
> *death, between prosperity and disaster.*
>
> *- Deuteronomy 30:15 (NLT)*

God is pleading with you to choose life. You get ONE word. Let your response be wholeheartedly: life!

Why? Because the word life has momentum and when we choose it, it leads to prosperity. That's VISION.

PROSPERITY WITH A PURPOSE

God has a purpose for our prosperity. When we understand and accept this, we will want to generate more income than we ever dreamed possible—that's VISION!

Our VISION will not just be to build a bigger home for ourselves, but to help others have housing. We'll not focus just on buying a boat for ourselves, but will desire to put a Bible into the hands of millions of people around the world. Our focus will be to give all people everywhere access to God's presence. Our focus will be on finishing the task of the Great Commission. Your focus will not be billions for yourself, but God's presence for billions of people.

In Matthew 28:18-20 (NLT), we read:

> *Jesus came and told his disciples, "I have been given all authority in heaven and on earth. Therefore, go and make disciples of all the nations, baptizing them in the name of the Father and the Son and the Holy Spirit. Teach these new disciples to obey all the commands I have given you. And be sure of this: I am with you always, even to the end of the age."*

This is referred to as the Great Commission. Jesus is identifying His mission and giving His followers an invitation to join Him in His mission by allowing Him to fulfill His mission through them.

In Matthew 24:14 (NLT), Jesus says:

> *And the Good News about the Kingdom will be preached throughout the whole world, so that all nations will hear it; and then the end will come.*

Jesus is saying that the end of earth will not happen until the Great Commission is finished.

All of a sudden the VISION for our life goes from man-size to God-size. You can feed your family, but only God can feed the multitudes. All of a sudden the VISION for our life depends on God instead of you. God is wanting to display His glory through your life. He wants to show off what He can accomplish. He wants you to depend on Him, not on yourself. Build it for Him, not yourself.

Colossians 1:15-16 (NLT) says,

> *"Christ is the visible image of the invisible God. He existed before anything was created and is supreme over all creation, for through him God created everything in the heavenly realms and on earth. He made the things we can see and the things we can't see—such as thrones, kingdoms, rulers, and authorities in the unseen world. Everything was created through him and for him."*

The sooner you accept God's VISION for your prosperity, the better your life will be.

A VISION OF PROSPERITY

If your VISION of prosperity includes only yourself, it will never happen. That is not prosperity. I encourage you to adhere to this principle: **true prosperity produces prosperity.** Real prosperity doesn't include corruption. True prosperity prospers everyone.

Throughout human history when a dictator prospers at the expense of the people, the result is always corruption and never prosperity. In the dictator's house it may look like prosperity, but it is always temporary.

Let your VISION of prosperity include EVERYONE prospering. Help others to prosper and you will prosper. The law of prosperity is as sure as the law of gravity.

God created words with momentum. Your word, the word God speaks over you, the word you prophesy over yourself and others, will:

1. Cast VISION
2. Instill VALUE
3. Identify WHY
4. Eliminate NOISE
5. Prosper EVERYONE

Words carry VISION from God. The words you impulse determine your path.

What's Your Word?

As we will see in the next chapter, words instill value. VISION is useless if it is not backed up with value.

*"And the Lord said to them, "Now listen to my **WORD**:*
If there were prophets among you, I, the Lord, would reveal myself in visions.
I would speak to them in dreams.' "

– Numbers 12:6 (NLT, paraphrase)

1. **RECEIVE:** What is God revealing to you?

2. **RESPOND:** What will you do differently as a result of what God is giving you?

3. **REPEAT:** Who can you share with about this chapter?

CHAPTER 6

What would have happened if God had said, "Let there be light," and there was no light? Can you imagine going through life in total darkness?

God said, "Let there be light" and then backed it up with VALUE. There was light. That's VALUE.

When God says, "now choose life," He backs it up with prosperity. That's VALUE.

There isn't a person on the planet that doesn't want VALUE. We all want to be of VALUE. We've been created with the need to feel valuable.

CONTRADICTION

Vision without VALUE is a contradiction to God's character and Word.

AMAZON

Amazon backs up their word BUY with quality products, competitive prices, and speedy delivery.

Imagine how much buying would be going on if Amazon sold cheap imitations that broke within twenty-four hours of buying them.

Can you imagine what would happen if all of a sudden Amazon was known to have the highest prices in the world? That the same TV cost $200 more through Amazon than it did everywhere else? No one would buy it.

Imagine if it took three weeks to receive everything you ordered on Amazon? You wouldn't be ordering much would you? Next day shipping is VALUE.

I think you get the point.

The reason Amazon is successful is that they backup their vision with VALUE.

APPLE

Imagine if it took a college degree to use Apple's camera on their iPhone? Instead of smarter, they made it harder. No one would be buying the iPhone for its camera.

Apple is backing up their word smart with VALUE and their customers are rewarding them.

From 1984-2004 Apple had very little brand recognition and growth. It wasn't until 2012 that the Apple brand really began to take off. Growth plateaued during 2014-2016, but soared in 2020 with 38 percent growth. (24)

Today, Apple is the number one brand in the world followed by Amazon, Microsoft, Google, and Samsung who round out the top five brands worldwide.

Valued at over $2 trillion in 2021, Apple is the most valuable technology company in the world. Apple was one of the first companies to switch to the graphical user interface (GUI) and saw success with the first Macintosh. Steve Jobs, the founder and CEO, was one of technology's first "rockstars." Jobs was one of the first people to sell hardware as more than a tool for work.

Over the years, Apple's phenomenal success lies in a well-planned vision and strategy that stretches far beyond simple desktop computing. The company's leadership innovated and added mobile devices and wearables into the product line. And in each new addition they pioneered, both performance and design remained key drivers and undeniable contributors to the brand's unprecedented and ongoing success.

As we all know, this level of accomplishment did not happen overnight. Apple has been around for decades before it became the first publicly traded U.S. company to hit $1 trillion in 2018. And again, it reached a whooping $2 trillion valuation just over two years later on Aug. 19, 2020.[25]

Apple's word, smart, instills VALUE.

CHICK-FIL-A

"It's my pleasure" has become a standard reply from Chick-fil-A employees. That's VALUE. What if Chick-fil-A's food didn't taste good? Can you imagine what would have happened if their sauces were gross?

Not only is Chick-fil-A a fast food restaurant, they offer healthy choices and make you feel good about eating at Chick-fil-A. That's VALUE.

Quality products and services at competitive prices are a VALUE. Clean restrooms are a VALUE. Fast and courteous service is a VALUE.

Vision is worthless if it is not backed up by VALUE.

We've all seen contestants who have a vision of winning American Idol or America's Got Talent, but they are tone deaf. All the vision in the world is useless if it's not backed up by VALUE.

God backs up His vision with VALUE in three ways:

1. Communication
2. Ease
3. Needs

COMMUNICATION

Check this out...

> *Now listen! Today I am giving you a choice between life and*
> *death, between prosperity and disaster.*
> *- Deuteronomy 30:15 (NLT)*

Hopefully you're starting to memorize this.

God is communicating. Clear and concise communication is VALUE. You may choose to reject God and His provision of life and prosperity, but it won't be because God failed to communicate effectively with you.

God starts by saying, "Now listen." There are two important points to consider here:

1. God speaks.
2. You're not deaf.

God has a vision for your life and He is effectively communicating it. It is clear. It is concise. You are able to hear God's vision. You are able to choose. You can choose life and prosperity or you can choose death and disaster. The choice is yours. That's communication. That's VALUE.

Many people and businesses have a great vision, but they fail to communicate it.

Communication is the number three challenge in life:

#1 Challenge in Life is Prosperity

#2 Challenge in Life is Vision

#3 Challenge in Life is Communication

As we saw in Chapter Three, it all starts with prosperity. The number one challenge in life is prosperity. Most people go out into life to make a profit. That's good. There is nothing wrong with making a profit, but profit is only a very small part of prosperity.

Mark 8:36 (KJV) says, "For what shall it profit a man, if he shall gain the whole world, and lose his own soul?"

You can have profit without prosperity and you can have prosperity without profit. In business, the goal is for profit and prosperity to come together. Profit without prosperity is tragic.

The number two challenge in life is vision. As we saw in Chapter Five, vision is so important. Vision drives prosperity. If our vision is only profit, then it is too small. God has promised us life and prosperity. Our vision should be prosperity. God created words with vision.

Communicating our vision is the number three challenge in life.

One thing I've learned in nonprofit management is that money follows VISION. The challenge is communication.

You can understand prosperity inside and out. You can have the best VISION in the world, but if you fail to communicate effectively, then it's of little VALUE.

Communication is VALUE.

Amazon's, Apple's, and Chick-fil-A's successes derive from their communications. They have VISION and they effectively communicate their visions.

AMAZON

Amazon's vision is you buying. Shopping can be fun, but Amazon has no prosperity until you buy. Before Amazon came on the scene, many brick-and-mortar stores like Walmart provided acres of products where you could go and shop. None of these products offered a "buy now" button. Instead of pulling up the product information on your smart device, you'd have to hold the physical product and read the box. There was no online search feature. Instead, you'd have to search the aisles, shelves, and racks in order to find the right product, size, and color. It took time. Sometimes it took a lot of time.

Amazon changed all that. They literally transitioned us from a culture of shopping into a culture of buying. Amazon backs up their vision with VALUE, and part of that VALUE is found in how they communicate their word: buy.

Other retailers have had to change how they communicate because of Amazon.

APPLE

Apple's vision is you being smart. Their vision is you being more productive and healthier. Their website is filled with beautiful photos that demonstrate how their products can improve your life. That's communication. Apple has a vision and they are effectively communicating it. That's VALUE.

CHICK-FIL-A

Chick-fil-A's vision is you eating more chicken. Responding with, "It's my pleasure" is ingrained into their culture. They are on a mission to make you feel good about eating fast food. They can articulate their vision in one word: eat. They back that up with VALUE. They effectively communicate this vision. The public loves their cute commercials with the cows that remind us to eat more chicken. Their other commercials offer heartwarming stories of kindness. It's all a very intentional communications strategy. That's VALUE.

Communication is the first way to back up your vision with VALUE. The second way is ease.

EASE

What do you notice?

> *Now listen! Today I am giving you a choice between life and death, between prosperity and disaster.*
>
> *- Deuteronomy 30:15 (NLT)*

It's so easy.

God could have written volumes of books on life and death. He could have imposed chapter tests. God has made it so easy. Choose life. It leads to prosperity. Or choose death. It leads to disaster.

Ease is VALUE.

We have a tendency to overcomplicate things. One of the consequences of the fall is the curse of complication. Things can get incredibly complicated when we refuse to make the right choices.

Another thing Amazon, Apple, and Chick-fil-A all have in common is that they never stop making it easier for everyone to experience their word.

AMAZON

Amazon is constantly making it easier for people to buy. Once you buy a product on Amazon, you can go back onto the Amazon website or app and within a few seconds find your previous order and buy again. That's easy.

Amazon has made delivery easy. They have made returns easy. Have you ever returned something and had to wait in line? Then, when you finally get up to the counter, they have trouble locating your order, the price, and processing the return? It can be frustrating to say the least. Amazon isn't perfect, but they have made buying easy.

APPLE

Apple works hard to make it easier for you to be smart. Earlier you'd have to get in line and wait all day for an opportunity to buy one of Apple's new iPhones. Now you can order online even before they are released. That's easy. Don't have the funds to pay in full? No problem, Apple offers payment plans. That's easy. Need support? Chat with Apple or have them call you. While Apple isn't perfect, they do hold a high VALUE of making it easy and, in every way, possible for you.

CHICK-FIL-A

Chick-fil-A makes it easy for you to eat.

Before the pandemic, Chick-fil-A had a bad record for having some of the slowest drive-thru times in the fast food world. When public dining rooms closed, something happened inside Chick-fil-A. They moved their employees out to their drive-thru. They set up multiple lanes with multiple employees taking orders, and then had other employees deliver the orders to the car windows. When many businesses saw their revenues drop because of the pandemic, Chick-fil-A saw a significant increase in their revenue. Their drive-thru times dramatically improved. The primary difference is that Chick-fil-A removed barriers and made it easier for people to eat. When other drive-thrus slowed down, Chick-fil-A's drive-thrus were wrapped around their properties. Chick-fil-A provided the VALUE of ease, and their customers rewarded them—a lot.

While none of these companies is perfect, they do everything they can to make it easier instead of harder.

It is important to remove all barriers and keep removing them. That's one of the primary challenges of business. Too many businesses fail because they are better at making it more complicated than easy. You'll want to remember this when we talk about the word "noise" in Chapter Eight.

God makes things very easy. Jesus even says, "Come to me, all you who are weary and burdened, and I will give you rest. Take my yoke upon you and learn from me, for I am gentle and humble in heart, and you will find rest for your souls. For my yoke is easy and my burden is light," Matthew 11:28-30 (NIV). That's easy!

Communication is the first way to back up your vision with VALUE. The second way is ease. The third way is by meeting felt needs.

NEEDS

What else do you notice?

> *Now listen! Today I am giving you a choice between life and*
> *death, between prosperity and disaster.*
>
> *- Deuteronomy 30:15 (NLT)*

Life and prosperity are felt needs we all have. God knows it. He backs up vision with VALUE.

1. God communicates.
2. God makes it easy.
3. God meets felt needs.

God VALUES people enough to meet felt needs. As we have seen, God created words with momentum. He created words with vision. He also created words with VALUE.

We could say, God makes words powerful. An explosion is powerful. Magic is powerful. What if the word light came with an explosive blast of light that went away like a firework? That would be light, but that wouldn't be valuable. Light is valuable because God meant for light to meet felt needs.

We've all heard the phrase: People don't care how much you know until they know how much you care. This originated with God. God is all-wise—omniscient. No one is wiser, but what makes Him so engaging is that God is also so caring. He genuinely meets felt needs.

God knows that a person's worth and dignity are more important than any product or service. Life is meaningless if not backed up with VALUE. Prosperity is VALUE. Why? Prosperity meets felt needs. God created words to bring VALUE. Prosperity brings VALUE to life. God teaches us to VALUE others enough to meet felt needs.

AMAZON

Amazon makes their customers feel like heroes. Picture a wife saying, "This is our last roll of toilet paper!" The husband opens his phone, scrolls to the Amazon app, and says, "Got more; being delivered tomorrow." Crisis avoided. He's now a hero!

Amazon is known as one of the industry leaders in using a fleet of environmentally friendly vehicles. Even their boxes smile. It's all an effort to meet felt needs.

APPLE

Apple knows everyone wants to feel smart, not dumb. Can you imagine what would happen if Apple Stores looked like a junkyard? If they were dirty and messy, Apple's story of success would be a very different story.

Apple's clean website and stores are very intentional. People love simple and clean environments. These felt needs are Apple's focus. The same with Chick-fil-A.

CHICK-FIL-A

Chick-fil-A knows that families have to eat on-the-go. They know that parents want to feel good about what they are feeding their kids. They know everyone wants dignity. They know everyone loves a good story of impact. Chick-fil-A is very intentional about meeting felt needs.

You need to back up your word with:

1. Communication
2. Ease
3. Needs

Are you effectively communicating your vision?

Are you doing everything you can to remove barriers?

Are you intentional about meeting felt needs?

Those who do prove VALUE.

God sets the example for backing up vision with VALUE.

- God communicates.
- God makes it easy.
- God meets felt needs.

We can see the outcome of these VALUES by looking at Amazon, Apple, and Chick-fil-A.

VISION is useless if it is not backed up with VALUE.

When God offers the vision of prosperity over your life, He backs it up with VALUE.

This is not:

- The power of positive thinking.
- Name it and claim it.
- Entitlement.
- Wishful thinking.
- A warm fuzzy without substance.
- Empty promises.

This is:

- Effective communication.
- Hear it and obey it.
- Grace freely given by God.
- Easy—fulfillment accomplished by God himself.

- Satisfaction of our felt needs.

- Promises backed up by God's character.

Your Word from God holds tremendous VALUE.

As valuable as all this is, ultimately what makes the words God speaks over you valuable is His authority.

I invite you to slowly read through these lyrics to the song "Authority" by Elevation Worship…

> *Creation knows the voice*
> *That spoke into the void*
> *The breath that brought the dust to life*
> *And sang the stars to form*
>
> *The darkness fears Your voice*
> *That drove it back before*
> *And though the night is long*
> *I know Your light will drive it back once more*
>
> *One word from You*
> *Things change on Your authority*
> *Your word, it's true*
> *Things change on Your authority*
> *Jesus, I know*
>
> *My fight is not my own*

Its end is in Your hands
I worship You because I know
All things must bow to Your command
We believe it

One word from You
Things change on Your authority
Your word, it's true
Things change on Your authority
One word; from You

Will Heaven not prevail and strongholds not be moved?
Will spirits not be silenced and cower at His rule?
For if my God is for me then what have I to fear?
And I will not deny Him the glory that is His
Will Heaven not prevail and strongholds not be moved?
Will spirits not be silenced and cower at His rule?
For if my God is for me then what have I to fear?
And I will not deny Him the glory that is His, oh
Heaven will prevail and strongholds will be moved
Shout it out

Spirits will be silenced and cower at His rule
I know my God is for me so what have I to fear?
For nothing will deny Him the glory that is His [26]

Songwriters: Brooke Ligertwood / Christopher Joel Brown /
Scott Ligertwood / Steven Furtick

"Authority" (Morning & Evening) lyrics © Capitol CMG Publishing, Essential Music Publishing

God's authority is His VALUE. I can say "live," but I have no authority to give you life. Jesus said, "I am the way, the truth, and the life" (John 14:6). He has the authority to give life. God backs up life with prosperity. That's VALUE.

God created words with momentum. Your word, the word God speaks over you, the word you prophesy over yourself and others, will:

1. Cast VISION
2. Instill VALUE
3. Identify WHY
4. Eliminate NOISE
5. Prosper EVERYONE

God created words with momentum. As we impulse them with our obedience, miracles only God can perform happen in our life. That's VALUE.

You choose your path one word at a time.

Words carry VALUE from God.
The words you act on determine your path.

What's Your Word?

In the next chapter we will see the VALUE in starting with "why."

"For you have been born again, but not to a life that will quickly end. Your new life will last forever because it comes from the eternal, living WORD of God. As the Scriptures say, 'People are like grass; their beauty is like a flower in the field. The grass withers and the flower fades. But the WORD of the Lord remains forever.'"

- 1 Peter 1:23-25 (NLT)

1. **RECEIVE:** What is God revealing to you?

2. **RESPOND:** What will you do differently as a result of what God is giving you?

3. **REPEAT:** Who can you share with about this chapter?

CHAPTER 7

As founder and executive director of Global Hope India, I used to exhaust people by telling them the 101 things we did in India. If you asked one donor, they would say we planted mango trees. Another person would say we train church-planting pastors. Still another person would say we care for orphans. Ask ten people about Global Hope India and you'd get ten different answers. Each answer would focus on what we do.

After reading Simon Sinek's book, *Start with Why*, we started focusing on our "WHY," which made our message not only clear and concise, but much more compelling. Instead of communicating 101 things we do in India, we started communicating our WHY. We believe everyone should have access to know about Jesus. Our WHY is to provide access for more people to hear about Jesus. We then focused on our three biggest whats: leader development, child development, and village development.

Your word, the word God speaks over you, the word you prophesy over yourself and others, will identify WHY.

Sinek is a British-American author and inspirational speaker. His first TED Talk in 2009—entitled WHY?—rose to become the third most-watched on TED.com, with over 40 million views. In his book, *Start with Why*, Sinek says, "People don't buy what you do. They buy WHY you do it."

Sinek shares how every company in the world knows what they do, which is WHY it's the first thing they tell people about. But rationale is a weak way of trying to get us to make decisions—probably the weakest of them all. And he says that's because emotions trump reason every time. When we make a decision based on a strong WHY, we own it.

Sinek says, only when we know WHY we do things will we feel a sense of belonging. That's WHY it's a much more powerful way of getting us to decide. Once we are sold on the cause of an idea, we'll go above and beyond to support it with our money and time. And in the cases of some movements, even with our lives.

Great leaders and companies naturally get this right. They start all communication with WHY they do things, eventually followed by how they do things. And then they finally reveal what it is they actually do.

Sinek says Apple is a great example. First, Apple tells us WHY they're here: to shake things up, then they tell us how: with easy-to-use, beautifully designed products. Finally, we find out what they make: computers, phones, watches, and tablets. By the time they get to their what, we're long sold on their cause and are ready to support them in every way we can.

According to Sinek, if you want to inspire others, start by telling them WHY you do things, instead of what you do, and you'll see a massive change in engagement. He also encourages businesses to hire people for their cause, not their craft, and watch business bloom.

Sinek points out that when you start with WHY, there's no need for manipulative sales tactics. These don't create trust; they evoke skepticism. He says that when we start with WHY and just communicate from the inside out, we'll build a group of customers that trust us. These true fans will always prefer our product over cheaper or even better solutions, because they believe in us and our WHY.

Understanding WHY is so important. Life without WHY is miserable.

God starts with WHY.

God says:

> *Now listen! Today I am giving you a choice between life and*
> *death, between prosperity and disaster.*
> - *Deuteronomy 30:15 (NLT)*

WHY choose life? Prosperity. It's that simple.

Dead people have no future opportunity of prosperity on earth. Life is over. We are either spending eternity with God or apart from God. If we are with God in heaven, we have eternal life and prosperity. We would never choose to return to our life on earth. Heaven is prosperity without problems. There's no disease, sickness, death, pain, or sadness in heaven (Revelation 21:4).

Prosperity doesn't start when we go to heaven. We are never more prosperous than when we are in the presence of God right here on earth. To be alive in Jesus Christ is to be alive in prosperity.

As Deuteronomy 30:15 communicates, prosperity starts the moment we say yes to life and goodbye to death. WHY take Jesus only for salvation? Life! WHY choose to live? Prosperity.

Life without the WHY of God's prosperity is a contradiction.

GOD STARTS WITH WHY

Perhaps you've noticed the subtitle to this book: Choosing your path one word at a time. WHY choose the word "life"? Because the word life leads to a path of prosperity. The one single word, life, has momentum, vision, and value. WHY choose life? Because of prosperity. God always starts with WHY.

As you can see, in ten chapters I am showing you ten very powerful words:

1. ONE
2. DISASTER
3. PROSPERITY
4. COLLISION
5. VISION
6. VALUE
7. WHY
8. NOISE
9. EVERYONE
10. WORD

When you're finished with this book you will know how to choose your words. Not just choose your word, but ultimately how to choose your path one word at a time.

God created words to identify WHY. As we activate, obey, and take action on a word's momentum, it identifies WHY.

WHY plant tomato seeds? You want to grow tomatoes.
WHY choose life? Prosperity.

KNOWING WHY IS POWERFUL

God's WHY makes your life:

1. Clear
2. Concise
3. Compelling

This is powerful and results in transformation.

CLEAR

Have you ever tried to follow instructions that were not clear? We're seeing that COLLISION is momentum plus action, that God created words with momentum, and that we choose our path as we take action on God's word. This is of little value if WHY we should act isn't clear.

Fortunately, God makes himself very clear!

God says, "Choose life." WHY? Because it's a path to prosperity. That's clear.

The Bible gives many clear instructions from God:

- Come
- Follow
- Love

- Serve
- Pray
- Give
- Stay
- Go

Sometimes we say or hear others say that knowing God's will is confusing. This identifies the battle between our will and God's will or our ways and God's ways. It's not that God is confusing, it is that we are not willing yet to obey.

Jesus says, "Come to me, all you who are weary and burdened, and I will give you rest. Take my yoke upon you and learn from me, for I am gentle and humble in heart, and you will find rest for your souls. For my yoke is easy and my burden is light," Matthew 11:28-30 (NIV).

Jesus says, "…my yoke is easy."

A yoke is a harness used in farming to partner two oxen together. Picture a capital B on its side. The head of one ox is put into one side of the yoke and the head of the other ox is put into the other side.

In the original language, the word for "easy" is used for easy, good, and kind. It means effortless, clear, simple, and straightforward. The opposite is complicated, hard, demanding, and exhausting.

When Jesus and the Bible say that God is easy, good, and kind, they are saying that God's WHY is clear.

It's the enemy of God, the devil, that lies, saying that following God is hard and confusing:

John 10:10 (NLT) identifies that Satan's purpose is to steal, kill, and destroy. Jesus' purpose is to give a rich and satisfying life.

John 8:44 (NLT) says, "Satan hates the truth. There is no truth in him. He is a liar and the father of lies."

Satan says, "God is not clear," but that is a lie.

God offers clear instructions for receiving salvation, help, bearing fruit, hearing God, and obeying God.

In John 2, when Jesus turned water into wine, Mary the mother of Jesus told the servants, "Do whatever he tells you." It seemed illogical to fill pots with water, but God had already used Mary to state a clear WHY: wine.

In Luke 5, when Jesus gave Simon a miraculous catch of fish, he instructed him, "Now go out and let down your nets to catch some fish." Simon was tired. The instructions seemed illogical, but Jesus had stated a very clear WHY: fish.

In John 5, when Jesus healed the man who had been lame for thirty-eight years, Jesus told him, "Stand up, pick up your mat, and walk!" The instructions were illogical, but the WHY was clear: walk.

In Luke 24:49, after the resurrection, Jesus meets with the disciples and says, "I will send the Holy Spirit, STAY here in Jerusalem until the Holy Spirit comes on you." Simple instructions: stay. WHY? To receive the Holy Spirit. That's clear.

CONCISE

The WHY given in each of the examples above is also concise.

1. Wine
2. Fish
3. Walk
4. Holy Spirit

All are forms of God's prosperity. God always starts with WHY.

John 3:16 (NIV) says, "For God so loved the world that he gave his one and only Son, that whoever believes in him shall not perish but have eternal life."

WHY did God give Jesus? Love.
WHY believe in Jesus? Eternal life.

God's WHY is clear, concise, and compelling.

COMPELLING

Have you ever been given clear and concise instructions that were not compelling? We all have.

Perhaps as we went through the Scriptures above, the reality of God always providing a clear WHY was eye-opening to you. It's easy to miss God's WHY. I did for decades. God's WHY is there. You just have to look for it. God always starts with WHY. If we will look, we can find God's clear WHYs throughout Scripture.

The enemy doesn't want us to see God's WHY. The Bible talks about this spiritual blindness:

"Satan, who is the god of this world, has blinded the minds of those who don't believe. They are unable to see the glorious light of the Good News. They don't understand this message about the glory of Christ, who is the exact likeness of God." - 2 Corinthians 4:4 (NLT)

Another way of saying this verse is that they don't see that the Good News is good. They don't see WHY they should trust Jesus.

One of the enemy's tactics is to blind us from God's WHY. We can overcome this trick by looking for God's WHY. God always starts with WHY. God's WHY is always clear, concise, and compelling.

God says we are transformed as we change our minds (Romans 12:2). And just as we need to accept and expect God's WHY to be clear, we also need to expect God's WHY to be compelling.

Prosperity is a compelling reason to live.

The enemy can't kill you physically. If the enemy can trick you into believing the only reason to live is to survive instead of to thrive, then he's able to rob you of God's WHY. Prosperity is much more compelling than survival until you get to heaven.

Psalms 34:8 (NLT) says, "Taste and see that the Lord is good. Oh, the joys of those who take refuge in him!"

Good taste is compelling. Joy is compelling.

God's WHY is clear, concise, and compelling. The enemy lies and doesn't want us to see the compelling qualities of God. Look for what's compelling and you'll find it.

John 3:16 says, "For God so loved the world that he gave . . ."

Love is compelling. Generosity is compelling.

God starts with WHY. It's that important.

Your word, the word God speaks over you, the word you prophesy over yourself and others, will identify WHY.

What's Your Word?

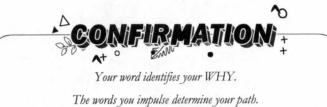

Your word identifies your WHY.

The words you impulse determine your path.

In the next chapter we will see how your word helps eliminate your noise.

*"Everything in the Scriptures is God's **Word**. All of it is useful for teaching and helping people and for correcting them and showing them how to live."*

- 2 Timothy 3:16 (CEV)

1. **RECEIVE:** What is God revealing to you?

2. **RESPOND:** What will you do differently as a result of what God is giving you?

3. **REPEAT:** Who can you share with about this chapter?

CHAPTER 8

When I wrote my first book, *Audacious Generosity*, I was surprised when my editor sent me an unexpected invoice for being over the word count. Their package I had paid for allowed up to 50,000 words. My manuscript was 75,000 words.

At the same time, a friend sent me a video of Donald Miller presenting his StoryBrand model. I'll talk more about him later. After watching the video, I immediately ordered his book, *Building a StoryBrand*. It arrived the next day, and I devoured it over the weekend. I remember halfway through feeling sick in my stomach. Miller made a clear case for eliminating your NOISE. My book was 75,000 words! I was about to have to pay more because it was 75,000 words. I knew publishing 75,000 words would be a big mistake! I was miserable. I remember thinking, "But how do I identify the NOISE and cut it out?"

It was miraculous! By the end of Miller's book, I knew exactly what I needed to do. On Monday I called my editor and said, "Give me a week and I'll send you a different manuscript." They agreed to wait. I went to work trimming out all the NOISE. If it didn't help to clearly make my points, it had to go.

In seven days, I trimmed the manuscript down from 75,000 words to 48,000 words. I went over the manuscript multiple times. I defended what stayed. I took out anything that wasn't absolutely necessary. I'm convinced that's when my book went from good to great!

I eliminated the NOISE. The pit in my stomach was gone. I became so excited and proud to publish *Audacious Generosity*. Eliminating the NOISE made the message clear and concise. I couldn't wait to send the revised manuscript to my editor. Not only did they void their invoice, but they agreed that it was so much better.

Being bombarded with so many words that we can't hear even one single word from God for our lives is a contradiction.

ELIMINATE YOUR NOISE

Donald Miller is an author, speaker, and business owner. He is the CEO of StoryBrand, a marketing company. In his book, *Building a Storybrand*,

Miller says the only thing your customers care about is if you can solve their problem. If you don't proclaim and demonstrate that you can guide them to be the hero in their story, they will find someone else who can.

Miller says, "It's important to establish what a customer wants early, before their brain has a chance to wander from your story." Miller offers practical guidance on helping you decide what your customer wants and helping them to know what they want. As such, Miller says, "What the customer wants should be obvious after five seconds on your website."

Miller gives the example of a painter who paints everything, so he builds a website showing people 101 things he will paint for them. He shares how it is exhausting for people to scroll through the 101 things listed on the painter's website. The potential customer is just looking for a painter, but the painter is so busy painting 101 things that he is failing to communicate, "We paint everything." It should be simple. Need a painter? We paint. Painting is a painter's what.

One practical tip Miller offers businesses with websites is that they only show 7-8 sentences of text per page. The website can offer deeper dives with links to read more. Miller says most websites violate this rule by posting paragraphs of text on their homepage and pages. Miller says when there is too much text visitors will stop reading and back out for survival.

Your word eliminates NOISE. In a universe filled with words, it brings one word into attention. A single word from God changes everything.

APPLE

Have you ever noticed how the Apple.com website offers lots of videos and photos but very few words? Apple gets it. They have eliminated their NOISE. You can click and find the longer text you need, but they don't use lengthy text on their homepage and other landing pages.

Other companies have learned this principle too, although most seem as though they have not. Actually, it is painful to reduce your message down to 7-8 sentences per webpage. Try it. Reducing your words is one of the most difficult exercises, but it can be one of the most rewarding exercises you'll ever perform. It's hard to eliminate your NOISE, but it is worth it.

CLARITY

Eliminating your NOISE brings clarity. It allows you to provide clear and concise communication. According to Donald Miller, God has created the human brain to allow your body to survive. If your brain detects something that will take energy away from your body, then it will back away. The term, "What's in it for me?" doesn't come from just a sin problem, but from how God created the brain to survive. If the brain can't quickly understand the story it is being told, it will back away.

Life is noisy. But God helps us to seek and gain clarity.

Long before Apple and other companies started eliminating their NOISE, God was already eliminating his NOISE. Now that sounds disrespectful to say that God could be noisy. It's not that we have to help

God through an exercise of choosing His words wisely. Actually, it's the other way around.

THE RED LETTER WORDS

The King James Bible (KJV) has 783,137 words. The New International Bible (NIV) has 727,969 words. [27]

The Old Testament has 929 chapters. It has 23,214 verses which comprise roughly 622,700 words. The New Testament consists of 260 chapters, divided into 7,959 verses or roughly 184,600 words. [28]

Both the Old Testament and New Testament hold equal importance. The Old Testament foretells Jesus and the gospel of salvation. The New Testament reveals Jesus and the gospel of salvation. The New Testament has less than a third of the words of the Old Testament. Wouldn't you expect it to be the other way around? God is clearly reducing His use of words to help our understanding and application.

Specifically, God isn't reducing as much as He is emphasizing certain words to make a point.

In John 14:26 (CEV), Jesus said, "But the Holy Spirit will come and help you, because the Father will send the Spirit to take my place. The Spirit will teach you everything and will remind you of what I said while I was with you."

This one verse results in God separating out the words Jesus spoke from all the other words of the Bible. This doesn't mean He deleted the other words or that they were not just as valuable to our understanding and application. They are. God is creating a focus to help us value the importance of the words Jesus spoke.

John 14:26 could have said that the Holy Spirit will teach us the complete Old Testament. And, He does. But God specifically calls to our attention that the Holy Spirit reminds us of what Jesus has spoken.

Many Bibles show the words of Jesus in red letters. These words of Jesus are found in what is referred to as the four gospels: Matthew, Mark, Luke, and John. These four books contain 83,680 words.

When the text of these four books is arranged side-by-side with a word-for-word merger in a parallel version, called The Synoptic Gospel, it contains only 65,460 words. This is 22 percent shorter in length.

Of the 65,460 words in this unified Gospel story, 31,426 words are the original words spoken by Jesus Christ. These words are identified as red letter words. Almost half of the words in the Gospels of Matthew, Mark, Luke, and John are the words of Jesus. [29]

BECOMING CLEAR AND CONCISE

Of the 730,000 words in the Bible, Jesus says in John 14:26 that the Father will send the Holy Spirit to remind us of the 31,426 words Jesus spoke.

Jesus commonly used these phrases:

- "Don't let your hearts be troubled!"
- "You have heard it said ... but I say to you ..."
- "Surely, Surely, I tell you..."
- "The Kingdom of heaven is closer than you think."

One in seven verses Jesus spoke contain references to money. He often used a reference to money to make a bigger point.

One of the most common topics of Jesus was the Kingdom of God. God's whole point is you in His presence and His presence in you. I suggest interchanging the word "kingdom" for "presence."

Jesus' primary message is that God's presence has come. Every time Jesus said, "the kingdom of God is at hand," he was standing in their midst. The whole point was the presence of God. Everything Jesus said is centered around God's presence.

It shouldn't surprise us that Jesus, who was God, taught mostly about God and His presence. From the very beginning of Jesus' ministry, the focus was on God establishing His presence on the earth.

Faith and salvation are also frequent topics of Jesus. These are a means to the presence of God. In earthly kingdoms, most subjects of the king rarely encountered (if ever) the ruler. In God's kingdom, we are uniquely empowered to accomplish our King's purposes by our King's living presence and personal guidance within us. We hold a unique hope because we are not subjects, servants, or even friends but have been adopted as children and inheritors. Let that sink in for a minute

One of Jesus' most frequently used words was the word "hear."

Jesus said many times throughout the gospels of Matthew, Mark, and Luke, "He who has ears to hear, let him hear."

LESS IS MORE

Life is short. The average lifespan worldwide is seventy-three years. That's dramatically increased over the last fifty years, but it is still short. You have days, not decades, to identify your word(s) for your life. Most of us drown ourselves and others with too much NOISE. Statements in sentences and paragraphs are helpful, but can be too wordy. God created words with momentum. Could you imagine how complicated life would be if God had created volumes of books with momentum? Fortunately, God didn't say:

> *Now listen! Today I am giving you a choice between this 899 page book or this 933 page book, between success and failure.*
> *- Deuteronomy 30:15 (NLT)*

No! He said:

> *Now listen! Today I am giving you a choice between life and death, between prosperity and disaster.*
> *- Deuteronomy 30:15 (NLT)*

God eliminated the NOISE for us. He created single individual words with momentum. God said let there be light and there was light. That's clarity. That's being clear and concise.

YOUR WORD ELIMINATES YOUR NOISE

The human brain has been created to quickly begin ignoring anything that's not useful for survival. There really is truth to the term: too much information. The brain processes millions of decisions each day and filters out more than 95 percent of the information we see, hear, and touch. It only keeps less than five percent required for our survival.

Most people say they don't use the math they learned in high school. Actually, most college graduates end up in careers outside their degrees. In fact, research shows that only 27 percent of college graduates landed a job closely related to their majors. (30)

Most information is wasted. It's NOISE to your brain created to focus on keeping your body alive. Survival takes eliminating the NOISE.

CONFIRMATION

Your word eliminates your NOISE.

The words you impulse determine your path.

What's Your Word?

In the next chapter we will see how your word prospers everyone.

*"But don't just listen to God's **WORD**. You must do what it says. Otherwise, you are only fooling yourselves. For if you listen to the word and don't obey, it is like glancing at your face in a mirror. You see yourself, walk away, and forget what you look like. But if you look carefully into the perfect law that sets you free, and if you do what it says and don't forget what you heard, then God will bless you for doing it."*

- James 1:22-25 (NLT)

1. RECEIVE: What is God revealing to you?

2. RESPOND: What will you do differently as a result of what God is giving you?

3. REPEAT: Who can you share with about this chapter?

CHAPTER 9

God says:

> *Now listen! Today I am giving you a choice between life and*
> *death, between prosperity and disaster.*
> *- Deuteronomy 30:15 (NLT)*

God makes it possible for us to choose our path one word at a time.

We can choose life or death, prosperity or disaster.

God created words with momentum. Your word, the word God speaks over you, the word you prophesy over yourself and others, will:

    1.   Cast VISION

2. Instill VALUE

3. Identify WHY

4. Eliminate NOISE

5. Prosper EVERYONE

This is the chapter where casting vision, instilling value, identifying why, and eliminating noise all come together. One reason: to prosper EVERYONE.

*A Word from God that isn't for EVERYONE is a
contradiction to the nature and character of God.*

GOD IS FOR EVERYONE

In Ephesians 4:5-6 (NLT), we read, "There is one Lord, one faith, one baptism, one God and Father of all, who is over all, in all, and living through all."

That's EVERYONE.

The people of Jesus' time saw firsthand that Jesus is not just for the wealthy, well-connected, or special people. Nope, the truth is—Jesus is for EVERYONE.

The Prophet Joel said, "I will pour out my Spirit upon all people. Your sons and daughters will prophesy. Your old men will dream dreams, and your young men will see visions," Joel 2:28 (NLT). The Holy Spirit is available to EVERYONE.

God the Father, Son, and Holy Spirit is for EVERYONE.

GOD'S LOVE IS FOR EVERYONE

John 3:16 says, "For God so loved the world." He could have said…

For God so loved:

- Senior management
- People of the same skin color
- One particular nation
- People with the same last name
- Shareholders
- Himself

But it literally says: God so loved the world. That's the whole world. That's EVERYONE.

If you're going to follow Christ, He's going to lead you to the word EVERYONE.

EVERYTHING GOD OFFERS IS FOR EVERYONE

Throughout human history, any movement to offer God to some but not to EVERYONE has failed.

- The Holocaust fails
- Slavery fails
- Oppression of women fails

Even if something not meant for EVERYONE seems to succeed on earth it will fail in eternity.

LIGHT IS FOR EVERYONE

God said, "Let there be light," and there was light. And as we read on, that light allows us to see everything else that God continues to create.

Speaking of Jesus, the disciple John wrote, "God sent a man, John the Baptist, to tell about the light so that EVERYONE might believe because of his testimony. John himself was not the light; he was simply a witness to tell about the light. The one who is the true light, who gives light to EVERYONE, was coming into the world," John 1:6-9 (NLT).

Matthew 5:15 (NLT) says, "No one lights a lamp and then puts it under a basket. Instead, a lamp is placed on a stand, where it gives light to EVERYONE in the house."

Light is for EVERYONE.

Actually, everything God does is for EVERYONE.

LIFE IS FOR EVERYONE

You did not choose to be born. Your mom and dad reproduced offspring and here you are. As we have seen, God says:

> *Now listen! Today I am giving you a choice between life and death, between prosperity and disaster.*
>
> *- Deuteronomy 30:15 (NLT)*

This is for EVERYONE. God has given you a choice to make. EVERYONE has the same choice to make between life and death. Sadly, some parents choose to take the life of their child. Whether we get to live or not, life is still a choice. EVERYONE has to decide whether they will choose life or death.

Deuteronomy 30:15 isn't just for those who read it, accept God, and believe it.

Life is offered for EVERYONE.

SALVATION IS FOR EVERYONE

If you only value salvation for yourself, then you are unaware of God as the giver of salvation. Jesus died for the whole world. That's EVERYONE.

A swimming pool in a five-star resort may be beautiful and luxurious, but it's not relaxing if someone is drowning in the pool while you're sitting there holding the life preserver. Salvation is not a gift only for you. It is a gift for EVERYONE. Once you've been given the gift of salvation it is meant to be shared with EVERYONE.

2 Peter 3:9 (NIV) says, "He is patient with you, not wanting anyone to perish, but EVERYONE to come to repentance."

As good as your salvation is, it gets even better when it is for EVERYONE.

MOMENTUM IS FOR EVERYONE

As we saw in Chapter Four, God has created words with momentum. Anyone who acts on the momentum God places into an individual word can reap the benefits or suffer the consequences of that word.

God hasn't created words to have momentum for just people of a certain skin color or last name.

God has created words to have momentum for EVERYONE who impulses that momentum.

GOD'S PROMISES ARE FOR EVERYONE

In Chapter Two I mentioned God's promise to Abraham. Let's take a deeper look at that promise:

> *The Lord had said to Abram, "Leave your native country, your relatives, and your father's family, and go to the land that I will show you. I will make you into a great nation. I will bless you and make you famous, and you will be a blessing to others. I will bless those who bless you and curse those who treat you with contempt. All the families on earth will be blessed through you."*
> *- Genesis 12:1-3 (NLT)*

Here God is calling Abraham and giving him this promise: I will bless you and make you a blessing.

The Bible has established that Abraham is our spiritual father:

> *"This is my covenant with you: I will make you the father of a multitude of nations! What's more, I am changing your name. It will no longer be Abram. Instead, you will be called Abraham, for you will be the father of many nations. I will make you extremely fruitful. Your descendants will become many nations, and kings will be among them! I will confirm my covenant with you and your descendants after you, from*

generation to generation. This is the everlasting covenant: I will
always be your God and the God of your descendants after you."

- Genesis 17:4-7 (NLT)

This is important. I hope you can hear this. Every follower of Jesus has been spiritually reborn into Abraham's family and, therefore, into Abraham's promise. Spiritually speaking, Abraham is your great, great, great, great, great, great…grandfather.

The same God is offering you this same covenant.

Here God is establishing that not only can He prosper you, but He can use you to prosper EVERYONE.

When God told Abraham, "I will bless you and make you a blessing," he was talking about you. God's blessings were not just for Abraham. God's blessings are for EVERYONE who activates His Word with their obedience.

ABRAHAM, WHAT'S YOUR WORD?

In essence, God was saying to Abraham, "I will give you my word and it will be a word for you and for EVERYONE".

What if Abraham had responded, "You can bless me but no one else"?

James 4:2-3 (NLT) says, "You don't have what you want because you don't ask God for it. And even when you ask, you don't get it because your motives are all wrong—you want only what will give you pleasure."

James identifies two reasons God may decide not to act:

1. We don't ask God.
2. We don't include EVERYONE.

Had Abraham responded, "You can bless me but no one else," it would have blocked God from blessing Abraham. God gave Abraham two options:

1. Bless no one and Abraham doesn't get blessed.
2. Bless EVERYONE and Abraham gets blessed.

Obviously, Abraham chose option two.

God gives us the same promise: I will prosper you and use you to prosper EVERYONE. It comes with two options:

1. Refuse to prosper EVERYONE and you'll not be prospered.
2. Prosper EVERYONE and you'll be prospered.

Jesus promises, we are more blessed when we give than when we receive (Acts 20:35). God can't prosper us the same if we only want prosperity for ourselves as He can when we want prosperity for EVERYONE.

Jesus is pointing to where the greatest blessings from God are reserved. We all want God to bless us. Few of us wake up in the morning, longing to prosper EVERYONE. We need to change that.

PROSPERITY IS FOR EVERYONE

God has created life to lead to prosperity. God has not offered only to bless the United States of America. God has offered prosperity to EVERYONE.

You can choose to impulse the word "life." When you do, not only you, but EVERYONE close to you reaps the benefit of prosperity.

With one single word, God can use you to prosper EVERYONE.

DAN PRICE PROSPERS EVERYONE

I love this example from Dan Price!

In 2015, CEO Dan Price cut his own salary by $1 million to be able to give his employees a pay raise. Price raised the salary of EVERYONE to at least $70,000 a year at Gravity Payments, a credit card processing company based in Seattle, Washington. Some critics thought Price was crazy and had just bankrupted the company, but now years later the company is thriving. [31]

In the past seven years the company has tripled its sales and doubled its employees. And Price is still paying all his employees at least $70,000 a year.

Price says he makes $70,000 a year too. And he says he had to downsize his life in order to pay his own bills. He sold a second home and tapped into his savings, but he made it work.

Andrew Hafenbrack says, "It does go against what people expect and what we usually see in terms of corporations and companies." Hafenbrack is the assistant professor of management and organization at the Foster School of Business at the University of Washington in Seattle.

According to the Economic Policy Institute, the average CEO's compensation is 320 times higher than the salaries of their typical workers.

Hafenbrack says, "This shows that isn't the only way for a company to be successful and profitable," and "Do you pay what you can get away with? Or do you pay what you think is ideal, or reasonable, or fair?"

Price says that despite the success his company has had with the policy, he wishes other companies would follow suit. I couldn't agree more.

"I would say that's the failure of this. You know, I feel like I've been shouting from the rooftops like, 'This works, this works, everybody should do it!' and zero big companies are following suit because the system values having the highest return with the lowest risk and the lowest amount of work," Price says.

In essence, Price believes that higher pay has resulted in loyal employees, which has contributed to Gravity's growth. As he put it, "Our turnover rate was cut in half, so when you have employees staying twice as long, their knowledge of how to help our customers skyrocketed over time and that's really what paid for the raise more so than my pay cut."

The company did take a hit during the COVID-19 pandemic, losing 55 percent of its business in March 2020. At one point, Price figured Gravity was only four months away from failing, but it bounced back after its employees voluntarily took a temporary pay cut.

Among the employees who volunteered were new parents and co-workers Carrie Chen and Alex Franklin.

"We reduced our salary to $40,000," Chen said.

"Yeah, I think we took each about somewhere around 60%," Franklin said.

Since then, both Chen's and Franklin's salaries are back to normal, and Gravity repaid them their lost wages that they had voluntarily given up.

Chen and Franklin just had a baby named Thomas. They said that Price's policy made it possible for them to begin and afford a family.

"We are right on track for the American dream, you know, we have a beautiful baby boy, a wonderful home, a beautiful life. We're not only just living, we're able to thrive," Chen said.

Baby Thomas is among one of 60 new additions to the company family over the past seven years. Price also claims the number of employees buying homes has gone up.

To repay Price for his sacrifices and for the dreams he has made possible, his employees decided to all chip in and buy him a car. A gesture that meant a lot to Price.

"My employees have done way more for me than I could ever do for them. So the fact that they wanted to get me such an unreal, amazing gift, it's pretty special. I don't know if I can put it into words," Price said.

"You could've afforded that with your old salary," Carter said.

"Yeah, that's true. I'm way happier now than I was before," Price replied. (32)

PROSPERING EVERYONE

Now, that is prospering EVERYONE. The truth is our words have the power to destroy. The opposite is true. Our words also have the power to prosper EVERYONE.

Long before Dan Price cut his salary to prosper all his employees, God had established a Biblical principle of blessing us and making us a blessing to EVERYONE.

YOUR WORD IS FOR EVERYONE

Let's say God gives you the word "favor." It's not just for you but for your marriage and family. It is for your business and church. It is for EVERYONE.

God is for EVERYONE.

He is not going to give you a word of blessing and tell you not to share it with others.

If God gives you the word "victory," He is not saying you will have victory while EVERYONE else fails. That's not a true victory.

Your word is not just God's promise for you, but for EVERYONE:

- Your family
- Your children
- Your grandchildren
- Your generation
- Your future generations
- Your church
- Your business
- Your clients
- Your students
- Your coworkers
- Your neighbors
- Your friends

- The people you come into contact with
- The people you invest in
- People far from God
- All nations
- EVERYONE

PROSPER EVERYONE

I can prosper myself without prospering you. I can't prosper you without prospering myself. That's true prosperity.

You can't be in the presence of God and stay selfish. When you're filled with God you're filled with His love for all people. You are secure, significant, and accepted in God's presence. Live moment by moment in God's presence long enough, and God will begin asking you, "What about others?"

This isn't an inconsideration to you. Your needs are met. You know God is an ever-present help in time of need (Psalm 46:1). You know that every guidance and provision you will ever need can be found today in the presence of God. So, what about others?

In Genesis 12:2, God told Abraham, "I will bless you and make you a blessing." This is true of you too. Jesus promises that as great as it is to be blessed by God, it is even greater to give God's blessings to others (Acts 20:34) [33]

With the confidence that God will meet your needs, you are free to consider the needs of EVERYONE. This allows you to make the needs of EVERYONE first and foremost in your life.

Allow God to exchange the concern for yourself with the concern for others. Remember that eternity is at stake for billions of lost souls without access to the Gospel. Let God transition your burden "by" people to a burden "for" people. God's strategy is audacious generosity through you.

SUCCESS IS FOR EVERYONE

When God was impressing upon me, "You can feed your family, but only I can feed the multitude," He wasn't saying that family and career aren't valuable. He was shifting my focus. Taking care of myself and my family focuses my attention on RECEIVING. Taking on God's mission focuses my attention on GIVING. This is where the greater blessings are found. Jesus promises it is more blessed to GIVE than to RECEIVE.

It is God's mission that brings fulfillment and satisfaction into your life. You have the capacity to feed your family. Only God can feed the multitudes. It is His mission that gets your focus off of yourself. It is His mission that forces your dependency off of the portion you can produce, and onto the miraculous portion God can produce. It is His mission that allows Him to perform miracles through you. [34]

Here's the point: At the end of your life, success will be measured in God's presence in your life and the lives of others more than money in your bank account.

God wants you, not your money. He is passionately pursuing you. God's whole point is His presence in you and you in His presence. The purpose of your life is the same. God's whole point for your life is His presence in you and you in His presence. This is true for you and for others. Your focus should be on pursuing the presence of God and helping others to pursue the presence of God.

God has promised that as we seek first His presence, HE will add in all these other things (Matthew 6:33). You focus on God's presence and let Him focus on the money in your bank account. Remember, Matthew 7:11 (NLT):

> *So if you sinful people know how to give good gifts to your children, how much more will your heavenly Father give good gifts to those who ask him.*

Don't dare think that if you focus on billions of lost souls instead of billions of dollars that your offspring are going to be left to starve. That would be corrupt! Corruption is prosperity at the expense of others. God is not a God of corruption! God has promised prosperity. True prosperity prospers EVERYONE. The truth is God cares more about the future of your offspring than you do. God, not you, created the earth to sustain itself before He created Adam and Eve (Genesis 1-3). Long before you were born and started your family, God already had a sustainability plan.

The good news of the Gospel is that, in Christ, you are 100 percent totally secure, significant, and accepted. You are free to focus on the needs of billions of lost souls and to let God take care of you and your offspring. Your loving heavenly Father has got your back. That's a done deal. You and your offspring can bank on that.

Here's the point: you focus on God prospering EVERYONE and let God focus on prospering you.

If you fear you have a bigger desire to prosper yourself than God does, then you seriously need to let the Holy Spirit guide you through a survey of the Bible. No one wants to prosper you more than your loving heavenly Father. No one! Not even you.

This is why in Chapter Three I said that prosperity is the number one challenge in life. I'm laying out the challenge. It is a very real challenge! Are we willing to focus on prospering EVERYONE and trust God to prosper us? Will we allow God to put us into a position where we MUST seek His presence day by day in our lives? Are we going to focus on getting billions of lost souls to heaven instead of billions of dollars into our bank accounts? Are we going to focus on finishing the tasks of the Great Commission or on building a name for ourselves?

It is possible to become a follower of Christ, receive God's gifts, but never hear God speak the word EVERYONE. Most Christians are not aware of God's word "EVERYONE." This represents more spiritual blindness from the enemy. The last thing the devil wants is for every Christian to take action on the word EVERYONE. If that happened, the Great Commission would be fulfilled immediately.

In Matthew 28:19-20 (NLT), Jesus said, "Therefore, go and make disciples of all the nations, baptizing them in the name of the Father and the Son and the Holy Spirit. Teach these new disciples to obey all the commands I have given you." That's EVERYONE.

And in Matthew 24:14 (NLT), Jesus says, "And the Good News about the Kingdom will be preached throughout the whole world, so that all nations will hear it; and then the end will come." That's EVERYONE.

Here, Jesus is saying once EVERYONE hears about Jesus then the end will come. Our blindness to God's word, EVERYONE, is what holds back the Great Commission.

I'm living proof, there are blessings of God awaiting for anyone who will take action on God's word EVERYONE. If you don't already, I wholeheartedly encourage you to begin asking God to show you His heart for EVERYONE. I dare you to begin seeing that everything God speaks over you, gives you, and wants to do through you is for EVERYONE.

Should you choose to activate God's words for only yourself, you'll be forfeiting 99 percent of its momentum.

Words have momentum for EVERYONE. Not just you.

CONFIRMATION

Your word prospers EVERYONE.

The words you impulse determine your path.

What's Your Word?

In the next chapter we will look at choosing your path one WORD at a time.

*"But I ask, have the people of Israel actually heard the message? Yes, they have: "The message has gone throughout the earth, and the **WORDS** to all the world."*

- Romans 10:18 (NLT)

1. RECEIVE: What is God revealing to you?

2. RESPOND: What will you do differently as a result of what God is giving you?

3. REPEAT: Who can you share with about this chapter?

CHAPTER 10

What's your WORD?

One single WORD.

It's time for you to hear God speak a word over you.

It's time for you to prophesy this word over yourself and others.

It's time for you to choose your path one word at a time.

If you haven't already, I encourage you to place the burden of identifying the word on God.

Momentum is always God's responsibility. It is never your responsibility. Remember what I shared in Chapter Four, it is always God that makes seeds grow. Your responsibility is to plant and water.

When it comes to words, God is responsible for the momentum. You are responsible to act on it. You choose whether to obey or not. It's your choice if you will harness this momentum for prosperity.

CONTRADICTION

Having knowledge of God's WORD but never taking one single WORD from God for your life is a contradiction to the very WORD of God.

YOU CAN CHOOSE YOUR WORD

1. God creates.
2. You choose.

It's that simple.

God has fulfilled His part.

If you haven't already, now you can begin to fulfill your part. Now you can choose.

Hopefully, by now you see the momentum God packs into single words. This momentum:

1. Casts VISION
2. Instills VALUE
3. Identifies WHY
4. Eliminates NOISE
5. Prosper EVERYONE

The word "life":

1. Casts VISION
2. Instills VALUE
3. Identifies WHY
4. Eliminates NOISE
5. Prospers EVERYONE

The opposite is also true:

The word "death":

1. Stops VISION
2. Diminishes VALUE
3. Questions WHY
4. Brings NOISE
5. Results in disaster for EVERYONE

Two entirely different paths! The word choice in the middle:

Life ◄——— choice ——► Death

Life leads to a path of prosperity.

Death leads to a path of disaster.

You choose your path one WORD at a time.

What's your WORD?

COMMONLY USED WORDS

Here's the most commonly used words in the Bible:

1. Lord (uses 7,000-8,000 times)
2. God (used 4,300 times)
3. Man (used 2,750 times)
4. Israel (used 2,750 times)
5. People (used 2,270 times) [35]

Here are the rest of the WORDs in the top 20:

6. King
7. Son
8. Men
9. House
10. Day
11. Children
12. Land
13. Things
14. Hand
15. Earth

16. Sons
17. Jerusalem
18. Jesus
19. City
20. Father

God created all these WORDs with momentum too:

- Accepted
- Blessing
- Chosen
- Cleansed
- Committed
- Exalted
- Favor
- Give
- Go
- Grace
- Grow
- Holy
- Kingdom
- Likeness
- Loved
- Made
- Multiply
- Presence
- Reverence

- Righteous
- Saved
- Secure
- Significant

What's your WORD?

YOU CAN CHANGE YOUR WORD

Do you believe anyone can change the WORDs they use? I do. I'm living proof. I grew up impacted by the WORDs:

1. God
2. Poor
3. Divorce
4. Adultery
5. Bondage
6. Broken
7. Dysfunctional
8. Anger
9. Bitterness
10. Conflict

By the grace of God, He has focused me rather on these WORDs:

1. Lord
2. Faith

3. Bible

4. Ministry

5. College

6. Courage

7. Freedom

8. Prosperity

9. Blessing

10. Holy Spirit

The outcomes are as different as night and day. Just because you are handed one list of words doesn't mean you have to keep those WORDs for the rest of your life. You decide. You. Not your mom, dad, family, culture, or heritage. You decide what WORDs you will act on. You decide if you will reap the consequences of disaster or the benefits of prosperity.

Growing up we sang, "Oh be careful little ears what you hear." You can't control what WORDs you hear, but you can control what WORDs you impulse.

Neither of my parents ever held college degrees. Because of the brokenness in my parents' marriage and the dysfunction in our family, higher education was not a value in our home.

When I was 17 years old, I attended a Gospel meeting where I committed my life to God. I prayed a simple prayer, "God, if you're real, I want to know it." Wow! Did God ever answer that prayer. I look back and the Holy Spirit came upon me and gave me a desire to be in God's WORD. I couldn't get enough. I read the Bible for hours. Within a few months I began to sense God saying that He had a plan for my life. Within six months I accepted God's calling into full-time Christian service. God immediately began guiding me to go to college.

The WORD college wasn't handed to me by my parents, but it is one WORD given to me by God.

I'm living proof that there isn't a WORD God can give you that He can't fulfill.

My parents never held a passport. They rarely traveled outside of the state of North Carolina. By the grace of God, I've flown more than a million miles to twenty-seven different countries. I've been to India fifty-one times. Go has been one of my WORDs.

YOU GET TO CHOOSE YOUR PATH

Throughout human history, certain WORDs have haunted certain groups of people, but they don't have to. Some groups of people have chosen to favor the WORD "death" and have experienced the disaster it brings.

Death has become a riptide in our culture:

1. The abortion of babies we consider to impede our personal life vision.
2. The rising tide of suicide death among those unable to match their lives to the culture's vision of an adequate life.

3. The increasing acceptance of "assisted" death in elders with terminal illness.

4. The astonishing surge in gun homicides—including mass shootings—by humans who are angry their lives don't match the vision this world has promised them.

The consequences to the WORD "death" are real. So are the benefits to the WORD "life". The good news is that WORDS really do have benefits we can activate when we choose to do so.

ASKING GOD FOR YOUR WORD

Perhaps you've thought, "What's Your WORD?" was my question for you. It is actually your question for God. It is God who created WORDs with momentum. It is God who has breathed life into you and given you the opportunity to impulse this momentum.

Perhaps you can learn all you can about impulsing the momentum of WORDs without ever having a living relationship with God, but that would be a disaster.

Jesus asked this question, "For what will it profit a man if he gains the whole world, and loses his own soul?" Mark 8:36 (NKJV)

The point of life isn't to act on the right WORDs, but to have intimacy with the Creator. The miracle isn't in the WORDs, it is in the God who spoke them. It would be a tragedy to act on WORDs and not The WORD.

The WORD is Jesus.

Look at what John 1:1-5 (NLT) says,

> *In the beginning the WORD already existed. The WORD was with God, and the WORD was God. He existed in the beginning with God. God created everything through him, and nothing was created except through him. The WORD gave life to everything that was created, and his life brought light to everyone. The light shines in the darkness, and the darkness can never extinguish it.*

John is introducing Jesus. John 1:14 (NLT) says,

> *So the WORD became human and made his home among us. He was full of unfailing love and faithfulness. And we have seen his glory, the glory of the Father's one and only Son.*

Jesus is the WORD. The WORD is Jesus. God has created WORDs with life—with momentum. We impulse this momentum as we hear and obey the WORDs of Jesus.

CHOOSE YOUR WORDS

As we have seen, if you choose the WORD "death" you will suffer the consequences of disaster. If you choose the WORD "life" you will reap the blessing of prosperity.

God has not said to some people that they can only suffer the consequences of WORDs, and that they are not allowed to reap the benefits of WORDs.

God has given everyone the same opportunity to either suffer the consequences of death or reap the benefits of life.

Many families suffer the consequences of WORDs like:

- bitterness
- hatred
- guns
- kill
- death
- sickness
- murder
- drugs
- violence
- anger
- bondage
- addiction
- depression
- oppression
- divorce

Those who act on these WORDs will suffer the consequences of these WORDs.

Many families reap the benefits of WORDs like:

- forgiveness
- family
- freedom
- love
- peace
- life
- education
- health
- marriage
- medicine
- faith
- hope
- future
- kindness
- grace

Those who act on these WORDs will reap the benefits of these WORDs. WORDs have momentum.

You didn't get to choose whether or not to be born, but you do get to choose whether you will suffer the consequences or reap the benefits of WORDs.

It is possible to change your path—one WORD at a time.

Perhaps your family has a history of acting on WORDs that lead to disaster. You can decide right now to start acting on WORDs that lead to prosperity. WORDs have momentum.

Deuteronomy 30:15 is before you:

> *Now listen! Today I am giving you a choice between life and death, between prosperity and disaster.*
> *- Deuteronomy 30:15 (NLT)*

You get to choose which WORDs to act on. The WORDs you choose do not just impact you, but EVERYONE. If you choose to act on the WORD "death," you and EVERYONE close to you will suffer the consequences of disaster. If you choose to act on the WORD "life," you and EVERYONE close to you will reap the benefits of prosperity.

GET YOUR WORD FROM GOD

Your WORD comes from God. What is He saying?

This tool will help narrow down your WORD:

Identifying Your Word

First, pray: "Heavenly Father, what's your word over my life?"

List up to twenty-five WORDs that best represent/
describe your values and dreams:

1.
2.
3.
4.
5.
6.
7.
8.
9.
10.
11.
12.
13.
14.
15.
16.
17.
18.
19.
20.
21.
22.
23.
24.
25.

Add WORDs God has been keeping before you. The objective is not to identify as many words as you can. If you think of more than twenty-five, then cross out some in order to keep the list to twenty-five or less.

List the top five toxic WORDs in your life:

Example:

Toxic Word		Your Word
Worthless	opposite:	Worthy
1.	opposite:	
2.	opposite:	
3.	opposite:	
4.	opposite:	
5.	opposite:	

Next, list the opposites. If you haven't already, consider adding these words to your top twenty-five words.

Now, move the top ten words to this list. No more than ten, please.

1.
2.
3.
4.

5.

6.

7.

8.

9.

10.

Now, narrow your list down to your top five words:

1.

2.

3.

4.

5.

Don't worry, you're not abandoning the other words. You are zeroing in on God's one single word for you to receive right now in your life.

List top three words:

1.

2.

3.

What's your word?

1.

Congratulations!

CHECK YOUR WORD

Now, check your word. Does it:

- Align with the whole word of God?
- Announce God's momentum?
- Declare God's vision?
- Instill God's value?
- Identify God's why?
- Eliminate noise?
- Prosper everyone?

ACT ON IT

Then:

- Hear God speak it over you.
- Act on it.
- Choose it.
- Obey it.

- Speak it over your life.

- Pray it.

- Expect it.

Psalm 1:1-3 (NLT) says, "Oh, the joys of those who do not follow the advice of the wicked, or stand around with sinners, or join in with mockers. But they delight in the law of the Lord, meditating on it day and night. They are like trees planted along the riverbank, bearing fruit each season. Their leaves never wither, and they prosper in all they do."

Law and WORD are used interchangeably. This passage says, "But they delight in the WORD spoken over them by God."

HEAR GOD SPEAK YOUR WORD

God is not human, that he should lie,
not a human being, that he should change his mind.
Does he speak and then not act?
Does he promise and not fulfill?

Numbers 23:19 (NIV)

WHAT'S YOUR WORD?

Write it here: _____

Date: _____

The word you impulse determines your path.

I encourage you to offer this prayer of thanksgiving and conviction to God:

Father, thank you for speaking Your Word. I here and now receive it from you.

MEDITATION ON YOUR WORD

"May the WORDs of my mouth and the meditation of my heart be pleasing to you, O Lord, my rock and my redeemer."
- Psalm 19:14 (NLT)

Let the Holy Spirit marinate you in God's WORD over your life.

Prosper in all they do.

Oh, the joys of those who do not
follow the advice of the wicked,

> *or stand around with sinners,*
> *or join in with mockers.*
> *But they delight in the law of the Lord,*
> *meditating on it day and night.*
> *They are like trees planted along the riverbank,*
> *bearing fruit each season.*
> *Their leaves never wither,*
> *and they prosper in all they do.*
>
> *-Psalm 1:1-3 (NLT)*

I encourage you to hear and claim God's promise over your life: They prosper in all they do.

Chew on it.

DO YOUR WORD

This means taking action.

In John 8:31-32 (NLT), we read, "Jesus said to the people who believed in him, "You are truly my disciples if you remain faithful to my teachings. And you will know the truth, and the truth will set you free."

You don't know the truth until you obey it.

Sometimes you keep asking God to explain it, but He keeps telling you to obey it.

I now realize the truth because I obeyed. Fortunately for all of us, God's gift of freedom always precedes our obedience, but obedience is where we experience that freedom.

DECLARE YOUR WORD

"All who declare that Jesus is the Son of God have God living in them, and they live in God."

- 1 John 4:15 (NLT)

To declare is to acknowledge possession of.

The Greek root WORD is: homologeó (hom-ol-og-eh'-o) which means to speak the same, to agree. It is used throughout the Bible for: (a) I promise, agree, (b) I confess, (c) I publicly declare, (d) I praise, celebrate.

To declare is to speak the same thing God has spoken.

To declare is to agree with what God has spoken. It is not to think maybe God will, but to acknowledge possession of it now.

To declare is to celebrate now.

PROPHESY YOUR WORD

Acts 2:17-18 (NLT) "In the last days,' God says, 'I will pour out my Spirit upon all people. Your sons and daughters will prophesy. Your young men will see visions, and your old men will dream dreams. In those days I will pour out my Spirit even on my servants—men and women alike— and they will prophesy."

Amos 3:7 (NLT): The Sovereign LORD never does anything until he reveals his plans to his servants the prophets.

God speaks through the Bible, prayer, believers, and circumstances to reveal Himself, His purposes, and His ways.

A PROPHET IS A SPOKESPERSON FROM GOD

A prophet speaks on behalf of God. A prophet (or seer) is one inspired by God through the Holy Spirit to deliver a message.

2 Peter 1:21 (NIV) says, "For prophecy never had its origin in the human will, but prophets, though human, spoke from God as they were carried along by the Holy Spirit."

Everyone who hears and repeats a WORD from God is a prophet. If not, then they should not speak on behalf of God.

A MESSAGE FROM GOD

Prophecy is a message from God. The prophet's message is called a prophecy. Prophecy is a revelation from God, not information about God. There's a big difference between revelation and information. Man can share information. Revelation comes from God. Man can only report on today. God can foretell tomorrow.

FORETELLING THE FUTURE

Jeremiah 29:11 (NIV): "For I know the plans I have for you," declares the LORD, "plans to prosper you and not to harm you, plans to give you hope and a future."

1. God knows the future.
2. God wants to reveal the future. Hope requires a future.

OUR RESPONSE

1. Hear what God says.
2. Repeat what God says.

This is prophecy.

WE ARE TO PROPHESY IN LOVE

1 Corinthians 13:1-2 (NLT): If I had the gift of prophecy, and if I understood all of God's secret plans and possessed all knowledge and if I had such faith that I could move mountains, but didn't love others, I would be nothing.

WE ARE TO SEEK TO PROPHESY

1 Corinthians 14:1 (NLT): Let love be your highest goal! But you should also desire the special abilities the Spirit gives—especially the ability to prophesy.

STRENGTH, ENCOURAGEMENT, & COMFORT

1 Corinthians 14:3 (NLT): But the one who prophesies strengthens others, encourages them, and comforts them.

INTIMACY

The point of prophecy is intimacy with God. It's closeness. It is a byproduct of a living relationship with God. It is not about the office of a Prophet. The focus is God, not the prophet.

Prophesy your WORD. The WORD results in prosperity.

YOUR WORD IS YOUR WEAPON

Today, we live in a world with plenty of WORDs, but no weapons. I don't mean guns and bombs. I mean having a single WORD from God. When you're poor without resources for college, but God speaks the word "college" over you, then the word "college" becomes a weapon over every doubt and skeptic. The same is true for words like "wanted," "loved," and "precious." Others might use opposite words about us, but when God speaks "wanted," "loved," and "precious" over us, these words become our weapons.

The Bible describes that we are in a spiritual war.

Ephesians 6:12 (NLT) says, "For we are not fighting against flesh-and-blood enemies, but against evil rulers and authorities of the unseen world, against mighty powers in this dark world, and against evil spirits in the heavenly places."

Speaking of the devil, 1 John 4:4 (NLT) says, "the Spirit who lives in you is greater than the spirit who lives in the world."

In Chapter Two I shared about our current mental health crisis. I pointed out how statistics show that suicide is a growing trend.

Right now, nearly half of all Americans are suffering from anxiety or other stress-related mental health conditions due to the global pandemic. (36)

Drug overdose deaths are up 30 percent, year-over-year. Over 96,700 people die from drug overdoses in a year. Opioids are a factor in seven out of every ten overdose deaths. Drug overdoses have killed almost a million people since 1999. (37)

Why are we losing?

We are fighting a war without weapons.

"For though we live in the world,
we do not wage war as the world does."

- 2 Corinthians 10:3 (NIV)

Your WORD from God is your weapon. One WORD from God has divine power to demolish strongholds.

Every WORD from God is a weapon. We only need one WORD from God to have a weapon.

ONE WORD IS ENOUGH

In 2 Kings 4:1-7 (NIV) we read about a widow with only one small jar of olive oil:

> *The wife of a man from the company of the prophets cried out to Elisha, "Your servant my husband is dead, and you know that he revered the Lord. But now his creditor is coming to take my two boys as his slaves."*
>
> *Elisha replied to her, "How can I help you? Tell me, what do you have in your house?"*
>
> *"Your servant has nothing there at all," she said, "except a small jar of olive oil."*
>
> *Elisha said, "Go around and ask all your neighbors for empty jars. Don't ask for just a few. Then go inside and shut the door*

behind you and your sons. Pour oil into all the jars, and as each
is filled, put it to one side."

She left him and shut the door behind her and her sons. They
brought the jars to her and she kept pouring. When all the jars
were full, she said to her son, "Bring me another one."

But he replied, "There is not a jar left." Then the oil stopped
flowing.

She went and told the man of God, and he said, "Go, sell the
oil and pay your debts. You and your sons can live on what is
left."

All she had was one small jar of olive oil. She received a miracle. One is enough.

In John 3:16 (NIV) we see that "For God so loved the world that he gave his one and only Son, that whoever believes in him shall not perish but have eternal life."

With his one and only son God offered eternal life to everyone. One is enough.

In 1 Samuel 17:40-50 (NIV) we find the story of David and Goliath:

Then he took his staff in his hand, chose five smooth stones from
the stream, put them in the pouch of his shepherd's bag and,
with his sling in his hand, approached the Philistine.

Meanwhile, the Philistine, with his shield bearer in front of him, kept coming closer to David. He looked David over and saw that he was little more than a boy, glowing with health and handsome, and he despised him. He said to David, "Am I a dog, that you come at me with sticks?" And the Philistine cursed David by his gods. 44 "Come here," he said, "and I'll give your flesh to the birds and the wild animals!"

David said to the Philistine, "You come against me with sword and spear and javelin, but I come against you in the name of the Lord Almighty, the God of the armies of Israel, whom you have defied. This day the Lord will deliver you into my hands, and I'll strike you down and cut off your head. This very day I will give the carcasses of the Philistine army to the birds and the wild animals, and the whole world will know that there is a God in Israel. All those gathered here will know that it is not by sword or spear that the Lord saves; for the battle is the Lord's, and he will give all of you into our hands."

As the Philistine moved closer to attack him, David ran quickly toward the battle line to meet him. Reaching into his bag and taking out a stone, he slung it and struck the Philistine on the forehead. The stone sank into his forehead, and he fell facedown on the ground.

So David triumphed over the Philistine with a sling and a stone; without a sword in his hand he struck down the Philistine and killed him.

One stone is all it took. One is enough.

Chapter Ten ends where Chapter One began: ONE.

All you need is one WORD from God.

You choose your WORD.
The WORDs you act on determines your path.

WHAT'S YOUR WORD?

What's Your WORD for Your Year?

What's Your WORD for Your Message?

What's Your WORD for Your Book?

What's Your WORD for Your Marriage?

What's Your WORD for Your Child?

What's Your WORD for Your Business?

What's Your WORD for Your Cancer?

"Listen to the WORD of the LORD"

- Jeremiah 2:4 (NLT)

1. RECEIVE: What is God revealing to you?

2. RESPOND: What will you do differently as a result of what God is giving you?

3. REPEAT: Who can you share with about this chapter?

CONCLUSION: I GIVE YOU ME

One word from God changes everything. Now you know the value of hearing God speak a single word over your life.

Nothing collides more than words. Every day there are COLLISIONS of disaster and prosperity all around us. The difference between the two is words:

1. ONE
2. DISASTER
3. PROSPERITY
4. COLLISION
5. VISION
6. VALUE
7. WHY
8. NOISE
9. EVERYONE
10. WORD

We started with one:

> *Now listen! Today I am giving you a choice between life and*
> *death, between prosperity and disaster.*
>
> *- Deuteronomy 30:15 (NLT)*

God is giving us a choice and waiting for us to respond with one word. We are to reply with either the word "life" or the word "death." God asks us to choose one.

The word death has momentum and leads down a path of disaster.

The word life has momentum and leads down a path of prosperity.

We choose which path we take by which word we act on.

When we activate, obey, and do death, we suffer the consequences of disaster.

When we activate, obey, and do life, we reap the benefits of prosperity.

The word God speaks over us, the word we prophesy over ourselves and others, will:

1. Cast VISION
2. Instill VALUE
3. Identify WHY
4. Eliminate NOISE
5. Prosper EVERYONE

In Chapter Ten we concluded with "WORD." We asked God, "What's your word over my life?"

You identified your word:

What's Your Word? _____

Congratulations on allowing God to speak this word over you!

I can't wait to hear how God uses this one word to reveal Himself to you. Please share with me now at kevin@kevinwhite.us. This is only the beginning. Over the next year you'll see your path change as a result of this word. I encourage you to allow God to have His way. Never stop learning all you can about applying this word to your life.

Perhaps God will give you a prayer word or focus word for each new year. Allow these words to become spiritual markers in your life as you experience God and join Him in His grand story on earth.

SURRENDER

I want to leave you with the word "surrender." I encourage you to surrender your word to God. Don't allow the enemy to tempt you to prove something or make something out of your word.

The success of "What's Your Word?" is not you having some magic power, waving a wand, and pronouncing "abracadabra." It's not about you creating as you speak.

God isn't looking for you to master a word. He is inviting you to experience Him.

A story is told of a country church with a bus ministry that picked up a little boy named Timmy and brought him to church one Sunday:

> Timmy came into the church with a dirty face, messy hair, and wearing ragged clothes. Apparently he had not been to church before. During the service he sat quietly observing everything.

> When it came time to collect the offering, Timmy noticed some men carrying bowls to the front of the church. He watched as each of these men gave their bowl to someone who put some money into it before passing it to someone else.

> After seeing two or three people put their offering into the bowl, Timmy became concerned because he didn't have any money. He carefully watched the plate go up and down the rows of people.

> Finally, it got to Timmy's row. The people sitting beside Timmy tried to pass the bowl around him, but Timmy took the plate and looked at it. The ushers grew concerned expecting he was about to reach in and take some of the offering for himself.

> All of a sudden Timmy took the plate and walked to the aisle. At this point everyone in the church was staring right at Timmy watching his every move. A few people gasped. Many people whispered among themselves.

That's when Timmy sat the offering plate on the floor and stepped into it. He looked up at the cross behind the preacher and said, "God, I don't have any money today. All I have is me. I give you me."

Needless to say, there wasn't a dry eye in the church. God sent Timmy to church that day to remind everyone of the true offering to God.

Romans 12:1 (NLT) says:

And so, dear brothers and sisters, I plead with you to give your bodies to God because of all he has done for you. Let them be a living and holy sacrifice—the kind he will find acceptable. This is truly the way to worship him.

I love these lyrics to this song, "I Give Myself Away," by William McDonald:

I give myself away
So You can use me

Here I am
Here I stand
Lord, my life is in your hands
Lord, I'm longing to see
Your desires revealed in me
I give myself away

Take my heart
Take my life
As a living sacrifice
All my dreams all my plans
Lord I place them in your hands

I give myself away
I belong to you
I give myself away
So You can use me
Lord I give myself away
My mind doesn't belong to me
I give myself away
So You can use me [38]

A surrendered heart is the ideal posture when answering "What's Your Word?" It's not a pursuit of perfection, but a posture of surrender.

I encourage you to stretch out your hands to God. That's surrender.

What God wants more than anything is you. We've talked extensively about how God has created words with momentum and how you have a choice to impulse this momentum. We discussed how to activate, obey, and put into action the momentum God has placed into words. As we discussed, the context is an intimate love relationship with God.

God wants more than obedience. He is looking for surrender. God wants all of you.

In the introduction I shared a few of the words God has spoken over my life. Words like:

- Presence
- Courage
- Catch
- Fill

These are words I have activated. Words that changed the path of my life forever. Words that have allowed me to experience God and join Him in His story around the world. Words that have resulted in countless miracles in my life.

In Chapter Ten I shared about the day I prayed, "God if you're real I want to know it," and how God radically answered that prayer. Six months after praying that prayer I attended a Christian conference. The final message was on "God's Call." At the end of the service an invitation was given for anyone who sensed God calling them into ministry to come forward for prayer. I went forward. I don't remember having seen Isaiah 6:8 before, but my prayer at 17 years old was basically, "Lord, Here am I. Send me."

I've prayed similar prayers like this throughout my life. Hopefully you have too.

On Sunday, December 8, 2019, I was at church. For over a month God had been laying on my heart to write. God spoke to me through Psalm 96:3 (NLT): "Publish his glorious deeds among the nations. Tell everyone about the amazing things he does." I was reluctantly questioning, "Why would anyone want to read my story?"

I had given my life to God decades earlier, but I had not given Him my story. That Sunday as the offering bowls were passed, I remember standing in the back with tears streaming down my face as I offered God His story through me. Once again, I surrendered. Once again, like Timmy, I said, "I give you me." I'll never forget that offering!

We, not our money, are the greatest offering we will ever give to God.

That was the year God spoke the word "courage" over me. I claimed that word, courage, as my word from God for 2020. I had no idea how much God was going to teach me about His gift of courage. God offered and I took courage to write my first book, *Audacious Generosity*. It took so much courage to publish it worldwide in November 2020. I shared about God's gift of courage in *Audacious Generosity*. God continues to offer me courage and I continue to take courage.

It took more courage when God led me to start writing my second book, *Get to the Point*. I published it in 2021. It is all about the word "presence." When I published "Get to the Point," not only did I publish a book, but I launched Spirit Media, a new company that is reinventing Christian Publishing. That's "catch," which was my word for 2021.

I'm writing *What's Your Word?* in 2022 and my word for 2022 is "fill." I keep hearing God say, "I will fill this house with greater glory" (Haggai 2:6-9) and "I will fill the nets with fish" (Luke 5:1-11). I'm learning to let God fill.

These are the words God has spoken over me. These are the words I am prophesying over myself, you, and others:

- Presence
- Courage
- Catch
- Fill

For me, the path of passionately pursuing God's <u>presence</u> has given me unlimited <u>courage</u> that I am now experiencing a miraculous <u>catch</u> whereby God <u>fills</u> my life with His glory.

This is choosing your path one word at a time.

I can't wait to ask God, "What's Your Word?" over my life every year for the rest of my life.

The same is true for you. You too can choose your path one word at a time.

I'm sharing this to encourage you that God isn't looking for us to master a word. He is inviting us to experience Him. God wants you, not just your obedience to a word or law. From the moment He formed you in your mother's womb, He has been pursuing an intimate love relationship with you.

Your word, the word God speaks over you, the word you prophesy over yourself and others, will allow you to encounter the living God of the universe like never before.

Your word is an invitation to experience God.

It is an invitation to join God in His story—in and through your life.

It is an opportunity to surrender your life to God.

It is an opportunity to surrender your path to God.

Living a life surrendered to God is not a one-time event. It's a daily journey. It's a path you choose one word at a time.

Choose your path one word at a time.

In the introduction I promised you, "By the end of the book we will have a beautiful piece of art."

That art piece is you. It is God's grand story in and through you.

Now you can choose God's path of prosperity for your life. Now you can identify and harness other words for God's glory and mission.

Now you can identify the words God has spoken over your lives and activate them. Each word is a true gift from God, He wants you to receive and benefit from His glory.

I encourage you to recommend this book to three people in the next twenty-four hours. The chapters are intentionally easy for you to recall as you share with others.

1. ONE
2. DISASTER
3. PROSPERITY
4. COLLISION
5. VISION
6. VALUE
7. WHY
8. NOISE
9. EVERYONE
10. WORD

Help others choose their path one word at a time.

Stay in touch at kevinwhite.us.

ENDNOTES

CHAPTER 1

(1) "How Many Words Are There in the Bible?" 2015. Word Count. https://wordcounter.net/blog/2015/12/08/10975_how-many-words-bible.html

CHAPTER 2

(2) Wilson Wong. 2021. "3 dead in murder-suicide over snow removal dispute, prosecutors say." NBC News. https://www.nbcnews.com/news/us-news/3-dead-murder-suicide-over-snow-removal-dispute-prosecutors-say-n1256599.

(3) Christine Cosgrove, "Murder-suicides in Elderly Rise - Depression." WebMD. Accessed June 18, 2022. https://www.webmd.com/depression/features/murder-suicides-in-elderly-rise; Alicia VanOrman and Beth Jarosz. 2016. "Suicide Replaces Homicide as Second-Leading Cause of Death Among U.S. Teenagers." Population Reference Bureau. https://www.prb.org/resources/suicide-replaces-homicide-as-second-leading-cause-of-death-among-u-s-teenagers/; "Murder-Suicide".Violence Policy Center. Accessed June 18, 2022. https://vpc.org/revealing-the-impacts-of-gun-violence/murder-suicide/.

(4) "Suicide". National Institute of Mental Health. Accessed June 18, 2022. https://www.nimh.nih.gov/health/statistics/suicide.

(5) Hannah Ritchie, Max Roser, and Esteban Ortiz. "Suicide." Our World in Data. Accessed June 18, 2022. https://ourworldindata.org/suicide.

(6) "One in 100 deaths is by suicide." 2021. WHO | World Health Organization. https://www.who.int/news/item/17-06-2021-one-in-100-deaths-is-by-suicide.

(7) Reis Thebault, Joe Fox, and Andrew Ba Tran. 2021. "Gun violence in 2021: Shootings in America are up and experts fear it may get worse." The Washington Post. https://www.washingtonpost.com/nation/2021/06/14/2021-gun-violence/.

(8) "Suicide". National Institute of Mental Health. Accessed June 18, 2022 https://www.nimh.nih.gov/health/statistics/suicide.

(9) Michael Fitch. 2019. "Helping you prosper: The Shalom principle." UHY Hacker Young. https://www.uhy-uk.com/insights/helping-you-prosper-shalom-principle.

CHAPTER 4

(10) Statista Research Department. 2022. "Fatal civil airliner accidents by region from 1945 through February 28, 2022." Statista. https://www.statista.com/statistics/262867/fatal-civil-airliner-accidents-since-1945-by-country-and-region/.

(11) "Train Accident Statistics." McAleer Law. Accessed June 18, 2022. https://www.mcaleerlaw.com/train-accident-statistics.html.

(12) "Road Traffic Injuries and Deaths—A Global Problem." Centers for Disease Control and Prevention. Accessed June 18, 2022. https://www.cdc.gov/injury/features/global-road-safety/index.html.

(13) Adam Mann. 2013. "Odds of Death by Asteroid? Lower Than Plane Crash, Higher Than Lightning." WIRED. https://www.wired.com/2013/02/asteroid-odds/.

(14) "What are the odds of dying in a tornado?" Ask The Odds. Accessed June 19, 2022. http://www.asktheodds.com/death/tornado-odds/.

(15) David Ropeik. "How Risky Is Flying?" PBS. Accessed June 19, 2022. https://www.pbs.org/wgbh/nova/planecrash/risky.html.

(16) "Flood Damage and Fatality Statistics." Flood Safety. Accessed June 20, 2022. https://www.floodsafety.com/national/life/statistics.htm.(17) "Odds of Dying." Injury Facts. Accessed June 20, 2022. https://injuryfacts.nsc.org/all-injuries/preventable-death-overview/odds-of-dying/.

(18) Laura J. Colker. "The Word Gap: The Early Years Make the Difference." NAEYC. Accessed June 20, 2022. https://www.naeyc.org/resources/pubs/tyc/feb2014/the-word-gap.

(19) Paul Petrone. 2017. "You Speak (at Least) 7,000 Words a Day. Here's How to Make Them Count." LinkedIn. https://www.linkedin.com/business/learning/blog/career-success-tips/you-speak-at-least-7-000-words-a-day-here-s-how-to-make-them.

(20) Kelli Catana. 2018. "This New Research On How Often Families Argue Will Make You Feel Much Better." Moms.com. https://www.moms.com/argue-with-kids-normal/.

(21) Kashyap Vyas. 2019. "Momentum in Physics: Newton's Laws of Motion, Collisions, and More." Interesting Engineering. https://interestingengineering.com/momentum-in-physics-newtons-laws-of-motion-collisions-and-more.

(22) James Gallagher. 2020. "Fertility rate: 'Jaw-dropping' global crash in children being born" BBC News. https://www.bbc.com/news/health-53409521.

(23) Samuel Rodenhizer. 2018. "'Though you can easily count the seeds in an apple; it's impossible to count the apples in a seed.'" Quotation Celebration. https://quotationcelebration.wordpress.com/2018/01/29/though-you-can-easily-count-the-seeds-in-an-apple-its-impossible-to-count-the-apples-in-a-seed/.

CHAPTER 6

(24) Timothy B Lee. 2015. "How Apple became the world's most valuable company." Vox. https://www.vox.com/2014/11/17/18076360/apple;

Felix Richter. 2021. "A Decade of Growth: Apple Thrived Under Tim Cook." Statista. https://www.statista.com/chart/25610/apple-growth-under-tim-cook/.

(25) Kif Leswing. 2022. "Apple becomes first US company to reach $3 trillion market cap." CNBC. https://www.cnbc.com/2022/01/03/apple-becomes-first-us-company-to-reach-3-trillion-market-cap.html.

(26) Songwriters: Brooke Ligertwood / Christopher Joel Brown / Scott Ligertwood / Steven Furtick
"Authority" (Morning & Evening) lyrics © Capitol CMG Publishing, Essential Music Publishing

CHAPTER 8

(27) "How Many Words Are There in the Bible?" 2015. Word Count. https://wordcounter.net/blog/2015/12/08/10975_how-many-words-bible.html.

(28) "How Many Pages Are There in the Bible?" 2016. Word Count. https://wordcounter.net/blog/2016/02/21/101241_how-many-pages-are-there-in-the-bible.html.

(29) "How Many Words of Jesus Christ are Red?" 2017. The Synoptic Gospel. https://synopticgospel.com/blog/how-many-words-of-jesus-christ-are-red/.

(30) Brad Plumer. 2013. "Only 27 percent of college grads have a job related to their major." The Washington Post. https://www.washingtonpost.com/news/wonk/wp/2013/05/20/only-27-percent-of-college-grads-have-a-job-related-to-their-major/.

CHAPTER 9

(31) "CEO on why giving all employees minimum salary of $70000 still "works" six years later: "Our turnover rate was cut in half."" 2021. CBS News. https://www.cbsnews.com/news/dan-price-gravity-payments-ceo-70000-employee-minimum-wage/.

(32) "CEO on why giving all employees minimum salary of $70000 still "works" six years later: "Our turnover rate was cut in half."" 2021. CBS News. https://www.cbsnews.com/news/dan-price-gravity-payments-ceo-70000-employee-minimum-wage/.

(33) Kevin White, "Get to the Point". 2021, 120.

(34) Kevin White, "Audacious Generosity". 2022, 42-43

CHAPTER 10

(35) "What is the most commonly used word in the Bible?" 2017. The Bible Answer. https://thebibleanswer.org/commonly-used-words-bible/.

(36) "Facts & Statistics." Anxiety and Depression Association of America, ADAA. Accessed June 20, 2022. https://adaa.org/understanding-anxiety/facts-statistics.

(37) "Drug Overdose Death Rates." National Center for Drug Abuse Statistics. Accessed June 20, 2022. https://drugabusestatistics.org/drug-overdose-deaths/.

(38) Source: LyricFind
Songwriters: W Mcdowell
I Give Myself Away lyrics © Fun Attic Music, LLC

YOUR DAILY DOSE OF COURAGE TO LIVE GENEROUSLY BLESSED.

FREE
($42.99/year value)

SUBSCRIBE TODAY

SUBSCRIBE TODAY
KEVINWHITE.US

THE KEVIN WHITE SHOW

NEW EPISODES EVERY TUESDAY

**HELPING YOU PROSPER
IN THE PRESENCE OF GOD**